Earth & the Wild Outdoors

THE GREAT OUTDOORS
A MIND-BLOWN™ SERIES FUN BOOK

1000+ Mind-Blowing Weird & Fun Facts, Myths, Legends, Stories +

I0102556

ISBN: 979-8-9938493-2-4
MIND-BLOWN™ ENTERTAINMENT & PUBLISHING TEAM
IN ASSOCIATION WITH WG COAKLEY PUBLISHING LLC
ILLUSTRATIONS: LUMEN GARY, ALDEN SKETCH, KAREN SATO
RESEARCHERS: B.G SCOUT, WILDER FACTUM, IAN PATEL, JO VAN
IMAGE ATTRIBUTION TO: FREEPIK — FLATICON.COM, ADOBE, NASA, USGS, NSF

PART OF THE MIND-BLOWN™ FUN BOOK SERIES
FIRST EDITION
PRINTED IN THE UNITED STATES

The Official Stamp of Awesome Weirdness

CONTENTS

CONTENTS

CONTENTS

CONTENTS

THE GREAT OUTDOORS

Weird & Fun Facts, Myths, Legends, Stories, Quizzes, Cartoons & More

This is NOT a sleepy nature textbook.

This is a **MIND-BLOWN** book, *Officially Stamped with Awesome Weirdness*, and packed with over **1000+** strange, funny, totally unexpected facts, trivia, myths, legends, quizzes & more about the world outside.

Inside, you'll find:

❖ **Weird Facts** -- quick-hit mind-blowers you can drop into any conversation

❖ **Myths & Legends** -- classic campfire stories and what's hiding underneath

❖ **Short Stories & Triva** -- feel like you're out on the trail & over-caffeinated

❖ **Fun Family Quizzes** -- prove-it rounds to see who actually paid attention

PLUS: Funny Cartoons & More

1

EARTH & THE WILD OUTDOORS

WARNING!

This book might cause:

✓ Sudden outbursts of "what???" and "no way"
✓ Unplanned recitals of facts during dinner & parties
✓ Parents being strangely competitive during quizzes

WEIRD & FUN FACTS
Earth & the Wild
Outdoors

Our atmosphere is about **300 miles thick**, but nearly all life survives in the **lowest 5 miles (1%)**. Why? because that's where breathable oxygen and weather systems exist.

✦ **Earth's crust** is thinner than an **apple's skin** when scaled to size — only **20–30 miles thick**, floating on molten rock.

✦ **Mauna Kea** in **Hawaii**, not Everest, is the tallest mountain on Earth — rising over **33,000 feet** from base to peak, most of it underwater.

✦ **Mount Everest** grows about 1.5 inches per year as the Indian tectonic plate slowly crashes under Asia.

✦ **Antarctica** holds 90% of Earth's freshwater ice, and satellites reveal dozens of hidden subglacial lakes beneath 2 miles of ice.

✦ **Earth's rotation is slowing** by about 1.8 milliseconds per century thanks to the Moon's gravitational drag on our oceans.

✦ **Lightning** hits Earth about **8 million times per day** because the planet acts like a giant **electrical generator**.

✦ The **Sahara Desert** was once a lush **green savanna** — Earth's tilt and monsoon cycles shift every **20,000 years**, flipping it between desert and grassland.

✦ The hottest temperature ever recorded was **134°F (56.7°C)** in **Death Valley**, a natural heat trap shaped like a basin.

✦ The coldest temperature ever recorded was **−144°F (−98°C)** in **Antarctica**, where dry air and long polar darkness super-cool the surface.

✦ Earth has over **3 trillion trees** — several times more than the estimated number of **stars in the Milky Way**.

✦ A single lightning bolt can heat the air to **five times hotter** than the Sun's surface, creating a powerful shockwave.

✦ Earth has over **1,500 active volcanoes**, most clustered along the **Ring of Fire** where tectonic plates collide.

✦ The **Mariana Trench** is deeper than **Mount Everest** is tall — plunging nearly **36,000 feet** beneath the Pacific.

✦ Over **80% of Earth's oceans** remain unexplored because extreme pressure destroys most equipment.

✦ Massive **earthquakes** can make days slightly shorter by shifting Earth's mass and **changing rotation speed**.

✦ The **Amazon rainforest** produces about **20% of Earth's fresh oxygen** through constant plant respiration.

✦ Some **sand dunes** actually **sing**, producing deep humming tones when millions of grains slide together.

✦ **Rogue waves** over **70 feet tall** have been confirmed by satellites — once dismissed as sailor myths.

✦ A typical **cumulus cloud** weighs **over one million pounds** — because all that fluff is condensed water.

✦ Earth experiences around **500,000 detectable earthquakes** each year, though most are too weak to feel.

✦ **Earth's core** is as hot as the **surface of the Sun**, heated by radioactive decay and leftover formation energy.

✦ The fastest wind ever recorded was **253 mph** during an **Australian cyclone**.

✦ The **Great Barrier Reef** is the world's largest **living structure** — big enough to be seen from space.

✦ Earth gains up to **40,000 tons** of **space dust** every year as tiny meteoroids burn up.

✦ **Greenland** isn't green, and **Iceland** isn't icy — early explorers used the names as **ancient marketing**.

✦ Only about **10% of Earth's species** are known — most live in oceans or remote rainforests.

✦ **Lake Baikal** in Siberia holds more freshwater than **all the Great Lakes combined** — and is the world's deepest lake.

✦ The **Namib Desert** is the world's **oldest desert** — at least **55 million years** of extreme dryness.

✦ **Veryovkina Cave** in Georgia plunges over **7,200 feet** — deeper than six **Empire State Buildings** stacked.

✦ Earth may have once had a **twin planet** — a Mars-sized world called **Theia** that collided with Earth to help form the **Moon**.

✦ **Volcanic lightning** is real — caused when ash particles **rub together** and build electrical charges during eruptions.

✦ The **Dead Sea** shrinks by over **3 feet per year** — evaporating faster than rivers can refill it.

✦ The world is running out of **sand** — construction uses far more than natural processes can replace.

✦ The **Amazon** loses around **10,000 square kilometers** of forest per year — mostly from farming and logging.

✦ Earth's **magnetic poles** move up to **40 miles per year** — the field constantly shifts due to molten metal flow.

✦ Some lakes can **explode** — like **Lake Nyos** (1986), where trapped CO_2 suddenly burst out and suffocated nearby villages.

✦ Earth's longest **mountain range** is underwater — the **Mid-Atlantic Ridge** stretches nearly **40,000 miles**.

✦ The world's largest **waterfall** is also underwater — the **Denmark Strait cataract**, where cold water plunges beneath warm water.

✦ ✦ **Hang Sơn Đoòng** in Vietnam is Earth's largest **cave chamber** — big enough to fit a **Boeing 747**.

✦ Earth has **rogue magnetic zones** where **compasses behave unpredictably** due to unusual underground minerals.

MYTHS – BUSTED
Earth & the Wild Outdoors

Nature has its own rules, and most of them don't match the stories we've heard growing up. From sky myths to desert myths to straight-up scientific plot twists, this is where we separate fact from fiction. Get ready — some of these are going to surprise you. Time to see what's real... and what's just campfire nonsense.

✓ **Myth #1: "The North Star is the brightest star."**
Fact: It only seems important because it marks true north. Polaris is actually around the 50th-brightest.

✓ **Myth #2: "Deserts are always hot."**
Fact: A desert is defined by dryness, not heat. Antarctica is technically Earth's largest desert.

✓ **Myth #3: "Earth's seasons come from distance to the Sun."**
Fact: Seasons come from Earth's 23.5° axial tilt. Earth is actually closest to the Sun in January.

✓ **Myth #4: "Mount Everest is closest to the Moon."**
Fact: Due to Earth's equatorial bulge, Mount Chimborazo is the true closest point to the moon.

✓ **Myth #5: "Lightning never strikes twice."**
Fact: It does — the Empire State Building is struck 50–100+ times per year.

✓ **Myth #6: "Earth's continents don't move."**
Fact: Tectonic plates drift inches per year. Africa is moving toward Europe.

✓ **Myth #7: "The Sahara has always been a desert."**
Fact: Every 20,000 years, shifting monsoons turn it into a green savanna.

✓ **Myth #8: "Earthquakes only happen at plate edges."**
Fact: The New Madrid quakes struck the central U.S., far from major fault

✓ **Myth #9: "The Amazon makes most oxygen."**
Fact: Most breathable oxygen comes from ocean plankton, not forests.

✓ **Myth #10: "The Moon only affects tides."**
Fact: Lunar gravity also slows Earth's rotation, stretching ancient 22-hour days into today's 24.

✓ **Myth #11: "Bears hibernate all winter long without waking."**
Fact: Bears don't truly hibernate. They enter a light torpor and often wake up, shift around, or even leave the den during warm spell

✓ **Myth #12: "Water swirling down a drain switches direction depending on the hemisphere."**
Fact: The Coriolis effect is way too weak for sinks or toilets. The swirl direction is controlled by the shape of the bowl and the plumbing.

✓ **Myth #13: "Rain smells because plants release oils."**
Fact: The classic "rain smell" comes mostly from geosmin, a chemical released by soil bacteria. Lightning helps spread it through the air.

✓ **Myth #14: "Cacti store clean drinking water for survival."**
Fact: Most cactus juice is acidic and can make you sick. Survival experts warn that drinking it usually makes dehydration worse.

LEGENDS
Earth & the Wild
LEGENDS Outdoors

Legends are funny things. They get passed around on trails and campsites, each person adding a little extra spice until nobody's sure where the truth ends and the stoy begins. Some of them started with something real. Others are pure campfire imagination that stuck because people liked telling them. Here we take a look at a few of the stories that refuse to die and see if there's anything real hiding.

The "Hum" — Earth's Unexplained Global Mystery

People around the world report a low, rumbling sound — called *The Hum* — heard only in certain outdoor locations. It's so real that scientists have recorded versions of it, yet nobody agrees on what causes it: underground vibrations? ocean pressure waves? something manmade? No single explanation fits every location.

The Lost City of Z — Hidden in the Amazon

Early explorers insisted a massive ancient city existed deep in the Amazon rainforest. For decades it was dismissed as fantasy... until modern lidar scans recently revealed buried geometric structures and roads under the jungle canopy.

It may not be "Z," but something big was definitely out there.

The Grinning Man — The Mothman's Outdoor Cousin

During the 1960s, hikers and campers around West Virginia reported a tall man in a reflective suit who smiled endlessly without blinking. Police, newspapers, and investigators all logged reports. Some thinkers connect him to the famous Mothman sightings — others say mass panic fueled the legend

The "Walking Forests" of Madagascar

Locals claim certain trees uproot themselves and move slowly across the landscape over the years. While botanists found no proof of literal walking, some species *do migrate* across soil by growing new roots on one side and letting the back half die.

The Mongolian Death Worm - Desert Horror Story

A legendary creature said to live in the Gobi Desert, described as a red, sausage-shaped worm that can kill at a distance. Explorers searched for decades and found nothing... but scientists admit the desert is so harsh that many species remain undocumented. No proof, but the legend refuses to die.

Hikers near Stockholm — a trick of light?

Hikers near Stockholm's forested trails claim to see a silver commuter train rushing through abandoned tracks — a model that was retired decades ago. Some say it's a trick of the light... others say it's a legend born because the real train *did* look eerie and unfinished.

The Kushtaka - Alaska's Shape-Shifting Wilderness Spirit

Tlingit legend tells of a creature that mimics human voices and lures people deeper into the wilderness. Many modern hikers report hearing someone calling for help in areas where nobody was found. A chilling blend of folklore and outdoor mystery.

The Devil's Footprints - Tracks Appearing Overnight

In 1855, hundreds of miles of hoof-shaped prints appeared across snow-covered fields in England — over houses, rivers, and walls. Even scientists couldn't explain how the tracks extended for such impossible distances. Outdoor legend gold.

The Smoky Mountain "Blue Mist"

Visitors to the Appalachian wilderness have long reported a strange blue glow in certain valleys at night. Modern science suggests it may be aerosols from local trees scattering light...

but the exact mechanism is still debated, keeping the legend alive.

The Vanishing Hitchhiker of National Parks
Outdoor lovers across North America share almost identical stories: a solitary hiker or hitchhiker is picked up on remote park roads — but vanishes when rescuers return to give aid. Rangers acknowledge the stories but chalk them up to stress + imagination. Still, the legend persists.

The Sun Dog Guardians (Scandinavia & Arctic Regions)
For centuries, Norse travelers believed the bright "mock suns" flanking the real sun on cold days were celestial guardians protecting those who ventured across frozen lands. These sun dogs are real atmospheric halos caused by ice crystals bending sunlight, but early explorers treated them as signs of safe passage.

The Great Thunderbirds (Native American Plains Tribes)
Plains cultures told of enormous sky-birds whose wingbeats created thunder and whose blinking eyes formed lightning. While symbolic in meaning, sightings of massive condors and storms merging on the horizon helped fuel the legend. Some early settlers wrote in journals that they "saw wings in the clouds."

The Naga Fireballs of the Mekong (Thailand & Laos)
Every autumn, glowing red orbs rise silently from the Mekong River and drift upward before fading. Locals long believed they were spirits of water serpents. Scientists still debate the cause — some propose marsh gases, others atmospheric plasma — but no explanation fully matches the phenomenon's timing and behavior.

The Fairy Rings of the Moorlands (UK & Northern Europe)
Shepherds across the moors warned that circular patches of impossibly lush grass appeared overnight where "dancing spirits" were said to gather. The rings are real — caused by expanding fungal colonies — but the perfect geometry and sudden appearance made them one of the oldest outdoor myths in Europe.

The Red Tide Moons of the Coast (Global Coastlines)

For centuries, fishermen described nights when waves glowed blood-red under the full moon, believing it signaled danger or monstrous sea creatures. The glow comes from bioluminescent plankton blooming in huge concentrations, lighting up the water with eerie red-orange flashes at each step or wave hit.

The Ice Ships of Antarctica

Early polar explorers wrote about massive "ships" drifting silently across the horizon — ghostly silhouettes with masts and hulls carved by nature. These were real icebergs sculpted by wind into ship-like shapes. The optical illusions under low Antarctic sun made them look like drifting ghost fleets.

The Glowworm Caves of Waitomo (New Zealand)

Māori stories speak of stars trapped beneath the earth, guiding spirits through the dark. Explorers later found the caves filled with millions of glowing blue points — bioluminescent larvae that light cavern ceilings like a false night sky. The resemblance is so perfect it fooled early visitors into believing starlight leaked through stone.

The Devil's Kettle Waterfall (Minnesota, USA)

For over a century, people believed half of the waterfall's flow simply vanished into the Earth — swallowed by some bottomless cavity. Objects dropped into the "disappearing side" never reappeared downstream. Only recently did researchers confirm the water does rejoin the river beneath the bedrock, but the exact path remains hidden.

The Sky Serpents of the Andes

High-altitude farmers told of long, snake-like shapes twisting across the sky during storms, believing they were weather spirits controlling the rains. These "sky serpents" are real — massive sprites (upper-atmospheric lightning bursts) that look like red, branching creatures flicking downward from space for milliseconds at a time.

The Ghost Forests of the Pacific Coast

Indigenous stories and early settlers spoke of drowned forests where tree trunks stood silently in the surf, as if the ocean had risen overnight. Geological studies later confirmed that massive earthquakes dropped entire coastlines by several feet in moments, allowing seawater to rush in and drown whole forests — preserving their trunks for centuries.

LEGEND: The Ice Ships of Antarctica — Explorers once swore ghostly 'ships' sailed the ice. FACT: They were wind-carved icebergs creating eerie illusions.

MIND-BLOWN™ Cartoons

DID YOU KNOW?

Did you know the Earth's magnetic field flips completely every few hundred thousand years? North becomes south, south becomes north, and compasses would point in the opposite direction. These "geomagnetic reversals" have happened hundreds of times — and the next flip is already long overdue.

Did you know some beaches are made entirely of green, pink, red, or jet-black sand?
The color depends on what nature grinds up: volcanic glass, tiny coral skeletons, crushed shells, rare minerals, or even microscopic life.

Did you know trees "talk" to each other underground?
Through a fungal network nicknamed the Wood Wide Web, trees share nutrients, warn neighbors of insect attacks, and help sick trees survive longer.

Did you know it rains diamonds on Neptune and Uranus?
Intense pressure deep inside those planets literally squeezes hydrocarbons into diamond crystals.

Did you know some deserts have lakes that appear and disappear almost overnight?
Wadis and playa lakes can go from bone-dry to mirror-smooth in a single rain burst, then vanish again within hours.

Did you know there are rivers that flow underneath Antarctica?
Dozens of hidden subglacial rivers move slowly under two miles of ice, reshaping the continent from below.

Did you know some mountains *hum*?

A few high ridgelines—like Mount Frissell in New England and parts of the Andes—produce a low-frequency vibration that humans usually can't hear, but instruments pick up as a constant "mountain drone." It's created by wind interacting with rock layers like a giant natural pipe organ.

Did you know the ground can "quake" without an earthquake?

They're called *non-tectonic tremors*—caused by sudden groundwater shifts, massive underground ice cracking, or even the collapse of unseen subterranean voids. They register on seismographs but happen nowhere near fault lines.

Did you know Earth has invisible "skylights" over active volcanoes?

Some volcanic vents create *thermal updraft windows*—columns of rising hot gas that punch holes through low clouds, leaving perfectly circular openings tens or hundreds of feet wide. Pilots call them "volcano eyes."

Did you know winds in some canyons blow *uphill at night* instead of down?

These rare **nocturnal inversion winds** happen in deep, narrow canyons where trapped cold air reverses the normal flow. The effect is so strong that campers sometimes feel a steady breeze traveling *up* the canyon while the surrounding landscape stays dead calm.

STORY MOMENT
Earth & the Wild Outdoors

STORY
MOMENT

Nature & Human-Made Wonders

You're standing on the cliff edge at sunrise, staring across a valley that looks too big to fit inside your mind. Fog hides the river below, and for a moment, the entire canyon looks like it's filled with silver smoke.

Then the sun hits the opposite ridge... and something unbelievable happens.

A perfect triangular shadow rises up into the air. Not across the ground... *straight up.* Like a mountain trying to make a copy of itself in the morning sky. You blink, rub your eyes, and it's still there.

A few seconds later, the fog shifts, and the "floating mountain" dissolves like a ghost leaning back into the clouds.

You laugh under your breath. Nature isn't showing off, that's just what it does when nobody's watching.

You turn around to make breakfast... just as your camping mug vibrates on the rock beside you. A low hum rolls through the stone ledge, deep and musical.

The cliff is singing.
Wind found the right crack at the right angle at the right moment.

Between floating mountains and humming cliffs, something hits you:

The world is full of wonders. Natural and human-made, that feel impossible until the moment you see them.

LEGEND: The Sun Dog Guardians — Travelers believed the twin 'mock suns' protected them.
FACT: They're atmospheric halos made by ice crystals.

MIND-BLOWN™ Cartoons

WEIRD & FUN OUTDOOR FACTS!

Looks soft! / That thing weighs over a million pounds.
FACT: A typical cumulus cloud weighs over one million pounds of condensed water.

HOOoooooom... / Is something under the sand?!
FACT: Some dunes 'sing' by vibrating when millions of grains slide together.

That can't be real!
FACT: Rogue waves over 70 feet tall have been confirmed by satellites.

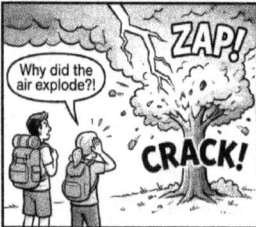

Why did the air explode?! / ZAP! / CRACK!
FACT: A single lightning bolt heats air five times hotter than the Sun's surface.

It's deeper than Everest is tall...? / Mariana Trench
FACT: The Mariana Trench plunges nearly 36,000 feet below the Pacific.

Huge quakes can change Earth's rotation?
FACT: Massive earthquakes can slightly shorten days by shifting Earth's mass.

MIND-BLOWN™ Cartoons

? QUIZ
Earth & the Wild Outdoors

QUIZ

Sometimes we all just need a quick breather and a few questions to wake the brain up. That's what this **Trivia Break** is for.

These aren't school-test questions, and nobody's grading you. They're the kind of oddball facts and curious details that make you stop for a second and think, "Huh... I didn't know that." **Take a guess, take a shot** ... enjoy the surprise.

1. What percentage of Earth's is covered by oceans?

A) 51%   B) 61%   C) 71%   D) 81%

2. Which continent has the most active volcanoes?

A) South America   B) Asia   C) Africa   D) Europe

3. What is the world's largest hot desert (by area)?

A) Sahara   B) Gobi   C) Great Victoria   D) Antarctica

4. Which lake is the deepest on Earth?

A) Lake Superior B) Lake Baikal C) Lake Tanganyika D) Crater Lake

5. Which natural landmark is so large it can be seen from space?

A) Amazon River   B) Grand Canyon   C) Great Barrier Reef   D) Mount Everest

6. Which U.S. national park experiences the most earthquakes?

A) Yosemite   B) Grand Teton   C) Yellowstone   D) Rocky Mountain

17

QUIZ ANSWERS
Earth & the Wild Outdoors

C) 71%

B) Asia

D) Antarctica

B) Lake Baikal

C) Great Barrier Reef

C) Yellowstone

"WEIRD & FUN OUTDOOR FACTS!"

These look carved!

Wind did all of this.

FACT: Wind erosion can sculpt rock into waves, mushrooms, and needles — nature's slow-motion

So which one is the longest?

Depends who measures it...

FACT: New mapping suggests the Amazon may actually beat the Nile for world's longest river.

Earth once looked like this?

FACT: During Snowball Earth, ice covered oceans from pole to pole.

Do tornadoes happen everywhere?

Every continent... except Antarctica.

FACT: Antarctica is too cold for the thunderstorms that produce tornadoes.

MIND-BLOWN™ Cartoons

2

WEATHER WONDERS

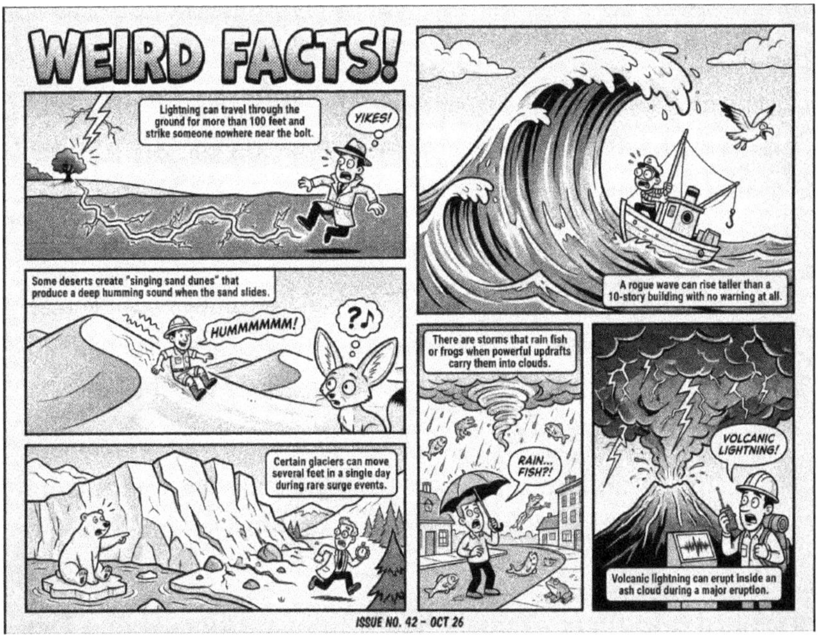

WEIRD & FUN FACTS —
Weather Wonders

MIND-BLOWN MOMENT

- **Raindrops aren't shaped like teardrops** — they're actually round or slightly flattened because **air pressure** pushes up on their bottoms as they fall.

- **Some raindrops fall at over 20 mph** because **large drops cut through the air with less drag** than tiny ones.

- **Clouds can weigh millions of pounds** because every tiny droplet adds up, even though **warm rising air keeps them suspended**.

- **Lightning heats the air to around 50,000°F** because the **electric charge superheats and expands the air instantly,** creating thunder.

- **Thunder is just exploding air** — lightning forces the air to **burst outward** at supersonic speed.

- **Most lightning never reaches the ground** — about 80% stays cloud-to-cloud because **storms mostly discharge electricity internally**.

- **Heat lightning isn't special** — it's just **distant lightning** that you can see but **can't hear** because thunder fades faster than light.

- **Double rainbows happen when light reflects twice inside raindrops**, flipping the second rainbow's colors **upside-down**.

- **Fog forms when the air can't hold any more moisture,** often **on clear nights** when the ground cools quickly.

- **Some fog can set off car alarms** because **tiny droplets scatter sound** and amplify vibrations.

- **Snowflakes form in dozens of shapes**, not just six-point stars, because **temperature and humidity** determine crystal structure.

- **It can snow at temperatures above freezing** because **snowflakes survive the fall** if the warm layer of air is thin.

- **Some deserts get snow** — the Atacama and Sahara have seen snowfall because **cold air masses can still reach dry regions**.

- **Thunderstorms can collapse suddenly** when **updrafts weaken**, cutting off the storm's energy source.

- **Hailstones grow in layers** because strong updrafts **toss them up and down** through different temperature zones.

- **Some hailstones grow larger than softballs** when storms have **powerful rotating updrafts** that keep them aloft longer.

- **Wind is just air trying to balance pressure differences**, rushing from **high pressure to low pressure**.

- **Wind gusts happen in bursts** because **surface friction** slows the air until sudden pockets break free.

- **A "sun shower" happens when rain falls from a cloud behind you** while sunlight shines from a **clear patch** in front.

- **Rainbows can appear at night** — they're called **moonbows**, created by bright moonlight acting like sunlight.

- **Some storms smell sweet** because raindrops release **plant oils** trapped in dry soil.

- **That fresh rain smell is called petrichor**, created when raindrops **kick up plant oils and soil compounds** into the air.

- **Hurricanes can push ocean water inland for miles** because strong winds **physically drive seawater upward** onto land.

- **Warm ocean water is hurricane fuel** — storms feed on **evaporating water vapor** that releases heat as it condenses.

- **A tornado's color depends on what it picks up** — dark soil, light dust, rain, or even snow.

- **Tornadoes can cross rivers and mountains** because they're driven by **wind shear and rotation**, not terrain.

- **Lightning can strike the same place repeatedly** because tall objects create **easy electrical pathways**.

- **Dust devils aren't mini tornadoes** — they form from **hot rising air**, not thunderstorms.

- **Volcanic lightning forms when ash particles collide**, building static electricity inside **volcanic plumes**.

- **Updrafts inside strong storms can exceed 100 mph**, lifting **hail, dust, insects, and sometimes small debris**.

- **Some clouds form perfectly round holes** called fall streak holes when **airplanes disturb super-cooled clouds**.

- **A "gust front" is a wind shift caused by cold air rushing out of a storm**, often **felt minutes before rain hits**.

- **Cold air sinks and warm air rises** because warm air is **less dense** and carries more energy.

- **Dry climates often see mirages** because **light bends** through layers of hot, uneven air.

- **Heat waves can bend distant sounds**, making things seem **louder or closer** than they are.

- **Lightning can travel through the ground** for dozens of feet because electricity **spreads out looking for a path**.

- **Some storms pulse** — weakening and strengthening in cycles as **updrafts and downdrafts battle for control**.

- **Snow rollers form when strong winds push sticky snow into spirals**, creating **natural snow "cinnamon rolls."**

- **Not all raindrops reach the ground** — some evaporate mid-air, creating **virga**, which looks like hanging curtains.

- **Jets can trigger lightning** when passing through charged clouds because they act as **giant moving conductors**.

- **Cloud shadows can stretch for miles** because low-angle sunlight produces **long atmospheric beams**.

- **Weather radar can mistake birds for storms** during migrations because **huge flocks reflect radar waves**.

- **Some lightning bolts shoot upward into space**, called **sprites**, triggered by powerful thunderstorms.

- **Hot pavement can create shimmering waves of "fake water"** because **heated air bends light** upward.

- **Cold winter air feels "heavy"** because it is — **molecules move more slowly**, making air denser.

- **Rainfall can look white in heavy storms** because thin sheets of water **scatter light evenly**.

- **Hail falls faster than rain** because ice is **denser and less affected by drag**.

- **Thunder can be felt as a vibration** when low frequencies **travel through the ground**.

- **Some storms create "gravity waves"** — ripples in the atmosphere caused by **air rising and falling like water**.

- **Sun dogs are bright spots beside the sun** created when **ice crystals** bend incoming light.

- **Antarctica has the strongest winds on Earth** because cold, dense air **drains downhill from its high interior**.

- **Fog can form even when humidity is below 100%** if tiny particles **help moisture condense** faster.

- **Warm fronts bring slow, steady rain** because warm air **slides over cooler air**, creating layered clouds.

- **Cold fronts bring fast, intense storms** because cold air **shoves warm air upward**, forming tall thunderheads.

- **Weather balloons burst at high altitude** because the **pressure outside drops**, letting the balloon expand until it pops.

- **A rainbow's center is always opposite the sun** because you see it through **light reflecting back at you**.

- **Triple rainbows are possible** but rare because they require **multiple internal reflections** inside raindrops.

- **Lightning rods don't "attract" lightning** — they **offer a safe path** when lightning is already nearby.

- **Desert dust can cause colorful sunsets** because tiny particles **scatter the red end of the spectrum**.

- **Sea breezes form when land heats faster than water**, pulling cooler air inland during the afternoon.

FACTS – WEATHER WONDERS!

24

MYTHS – BUSTED
Weather Wonders

✓ **Myth #1: "Tornadoes can't cross rivers or mountains."**
Fact: Tornadoes don't care about terrain. Their path is controlled by **wind shear and rotation**, not what's underneath them.

✓ **Myth #2: "Lightning never strikes the same place twice."**
Fact: It strikes preferred spots **over and over**, especially tall buildings where the electrical path is easiest.

✓ **Myth #3: "Cold weather means it can't snow."**
Fact: Snow can fall at extremely low temperatures as long as there's **enough moisture** in the air. Antarctica proves it.

✓ **Myth #4: "Thunderstorms always mean lots of lightning."**
Fact: Some massive storms barely produce lightning because they lack the **strong updrafts and ice crystals** needed for electrical charge.

✓ **Myth #5: "Hurricanes only form in tropical heat."**
Fact: Most do, but some **hybrid storms** form from frontal systems when the atmosphere releases energy in different ways.

✓ **Myth #6: "Heat lightning is a special kind of lightning."**
Fact: It's just **distant lightning** from a far-off storm. You can see the flash, but the thunder dies out before it reaches you.

✓ **Myth #7: "If a tornado isn't touching the ground, it's harmless."**
Fact: A funnel cloud can drop suddenly. The **rotating column above** is already dangerous and can produce damage without a visible ground touch.

✓ **Myth #8: "Large raindrops mean a storm is getting weaker."**
Fact: Big drops actually signal **strong updrafts breaking down**, which often means the storm is preparing to collapse or shift.

✓ **Myth #9: "Rain follows the farmer's plow."**
Fact: Old saying, but wrong. What farmers noticed was **dust rising**, which sometimes coincided with incoming fronts.

✓ **Myth #10: "Weather forecasts are just guesses."**
Fact: Modern forecasting relies on **millions of data points**, satellites, radar, and supercomputers — accuracy has improved dramatically, especially within 1–3 days.

"The sun did not shine. It was too wet to play. We sat in the house. All that cold, cold, wet day"
- Dr. Seuss

LEGENDS
Weather Wonders

LEGENDS

The Sky Whistler Storms

Coastal towns once told of storms that "whistled" before they arrived — high, trembling notes drifting through the air long before thunder. Sailors believed the sound came from spirits warning them to get inland. Meteorologists later learned the noise came from powerful wind shear sliding across cliff faces, creating flute-like tones that carried miles ahead of the storm.

The Lightning That Followed Travelers

In the Great Plains, early settlers claimed a bolt of "roaming lightning" stalked them across open fields, flickering behind their wagons like a pale shadow. The phenomenon was actually St. Elmo's fire — charged air glowing around metal tools, wheels, and even people's hair — but to tired travelers under a black sky, it looked like lightning with intent.

The Frozen Voices of the North

Arctic explorers once insisted that during still winter nights, they heard faint voices in the air — whispering, laughing, or calling out from empty tundra. Inuit hunters explained that drifting ice can crack miles away and the sound travels across frozen surfaces with uncanny clarity, arriving at camp like human speech. The effect was so convincing that some expeditions wrote about "ghost camps" in their journals.

The Storm That Chased the Lighthouse

Keepers along the rugged coasts of Norway told of a storm cloud that "followed" them whenever they walked between stations. The cloud seemed low, dark, and intelligent, hugging the ground like a living shadow. The truth was a rare type of fogbank — warm sea air hitting cold stone — that forms a mobile, swirling mass that moves at the exact pace of nearby warm bodies.

The Fire Rain of the Outback

Australian ranchers once described storms that rained "fire," claiming glowing sparks fell from the sky and burned the ground in tiny marks. The real cause was dry lightning striking superheated sand, sending molten grains flying in arcs that look like falling embers. From a distance, especially at dusk, it appeared as though the storm itself was throwing fire.

The Soundless Tornado

Farmers in early Kansas swore a tornado once appeared silently, without the roaring freight-train sound everyone expected. It moved across fields like a gray ghost, picking up dust and debris but making almost no noise. Meteorologists eventually learned that under rare conditions — perfect humidity, wind alignment, and terrain — a tornado's rotational roar can be muted. To those who witnessed it, silence was far more terrifying than thunder.

DID YOU KNOW?
Weather Wonders

Did you know lightning can strike the *same place* hundreds of times a year?

There's a spot in Venezuela called **Catatumbo** where storms rage almost nightly, producing more lightning than anywhere else on Earth. Pilots used it as a natural lighthouse long before GPS existed.

Did you know raindrops *aren't shaped like teardrops*?

Real raindrops start out round, then flatten into a shape that looks more like a **hamburger bun** as air pressure builds beneath them during freefall.

Did you know the stratosphere can create *rainbow-colored clouds* that look unreal?

These rare **nacreous clouds** glow like oil slicks at sunset and form only in the coldest places on Earth — mainly Antarctica, where temperatures drop below −112°F.

Did you know thunder can travel *20 miles* from its source?

Cold, dense air carries low-frequency sound far more efficiently, which is why you sometimes hear thunder long after the storm has passed or when the sky seems completely clear.

Did you know some snowflakes contain *microscopic meteor dust*?

Tiny cosmic particles drifting through the atmosphere get trapped inside forming ice crystals — meaning some snow literally contains **pieces of space**.

Did you know the largest hailstone ever recorded weighed nearly *two pounds*?

It fell over Bangladesh in 1986, causing widespread injuries. Modern research shows that powerful updrafts in supercell storms can keep hail aloft long enough to grow **bigger than baseballs**.

Lightning can strike from clear blue sky up to 20–25 miles from a storm. These are **"bolt from the blue"** strikes caused by strong electrical fields.

A lighting bolt can travel 300 miles?!

The longest "megaflash" ever recorded stretched across multiple states.

MIND-BLOWN

STORY MOMENT
Weather Wonders

I've seen plenty of storms, but only once have I seen the sky turn green. And let me tell you, it'll make you stop what you are doing.

I was on a prairie outside Cheyenne, camping out for the night. Big storm clouds had been building all afternoon. The kind that stack up like giant anvils and make you wonder if you should've picked a campsite with a roof.

Right after the sun dipped, everything around me went dim in this strange, underwater way. I looked up and the clouds were glowing green. Not neon, not sci-fi green, more like the color of a deep pond when the light hits it just right. I actually blinked a few times thinking my eyes were messed up.

They weren't, because a herd of pronghorn nearby all froze at the exact same time and stared at the sky. That's never a good sign.

The wind picked up real suddenly. Warm, dusty, and carrying that electric smell that always shows up when the atmosphere is getting stirred up. Later I found out that green skies sometimes happen when the sun hits storm clouds packed full of ice. But standing there, it felt like the sky was glowing from the inside.

Lightning flashed inside the clouds, lighting up the green like someone was flicking a giant light switch. One blast hit close enough that the ground shivered under my boots. Then came the hail — little ice marbles pelting everything in sight. It sounded like someone dumping a bucket of gravel on my tent.

And then, just as fast as it turned on, it shut off. Sky went back to normal. The pronghorn casually started grazing again like nothing weird had happened.

"WEIRD FACTS!"

QUIZ
Weather Wonders

QUIZ

Multiple Choice

1. What makes lightning so incredibly hot?
A. Friction with clouds
B. Compression of air during the electrical discharge
C. Heat from the Sun
D. Wind speeds inside the storm

2. Why do hailstones grow in layers?
A. They melt and refreeze on the ground
B. They form in warm air only
C. Updrafts lift them repeatedly through different temperature zones
D. Lightning fuses them together

3. What causes the "calm before the storm"?
A. The storm blocks sunlight
B. Air is pulled inward toward the approaching system
C. The storm loses power
D. The wind is too cold to move

4. Why does thunder rumble instead of making one single sound?
A. Mountains absorb the noise
B. Lightning branches in many directions
C. Clouds muffle the sound
D. It bounces off the ground

5. What creates a double rainbow?
A. Two storms at once
B. Light bending twice inside raindrops

C. Cold air behind the storm
D. Ice crystals in the sky

6. Why can hurricanes suddenly weaken when they reach land?
A. Land cools them instantly
B. They lose warm ocean water as a fuel source
C. Trees block the wind
D. Pressure disappears

7. What causes heat waves to appear as "shimmering water" on roads?
A. Pollution
B. Light bending through layers of hot rising air
C. Reflection of clouds
D. Melting asphalt

Fill-In-The-Blank

1. The smell of rain is called _____.

2. A rainbow is always directly opposite the _____.

3. When rain evaporates before hitting the ground, it's called _____.

4. Lightning that strikes far from a storm and appears on clear sky is called "_____ from the blue."

5. The fast-moving river of air that steers storms across continents is the _____.

6. Ice crystals bending sunlight into bright spots near the sun are called _____.

7. A sudden blast of cold air pushed out of a collapsing storm is known as a _____.

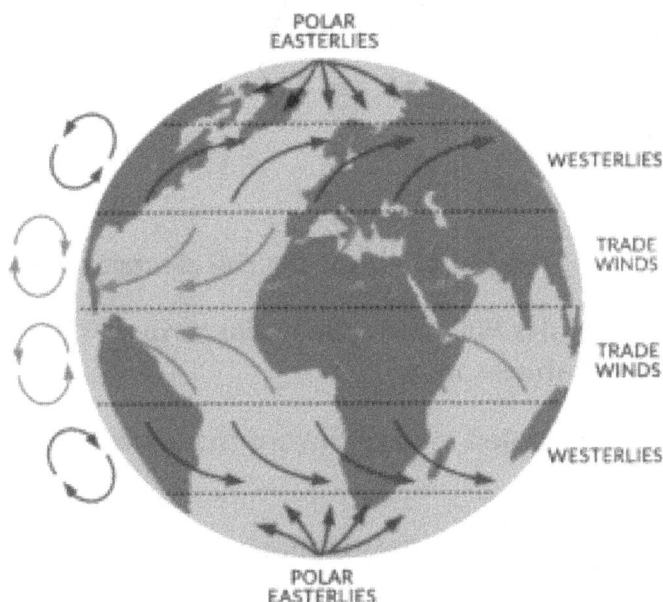

The **Coriolis effect** is the deflection of air because of Earth's rotation. In the northern hemisphere, air deflects to the right. But in the southern hemisphere, air veers to the left. This impacts air circulation, weather patterns, and ocean currents.

From 0-30° latitude, Hadley cells carry water vapor from the oceans at the equator. Then, it provides rain until about 30° latitude when the cell loses most of its moisture. So this is why the equator area is damp and moist. But at about 30° latitude, the air is much dryer.

Then at 50-60° latitude, it's a subpolar low within the Ferrel cell. Air moves north at 30° latitude, then comes down at 60° latitude north. Air deflects from the Coriolis effect causing the Westerlies to move east to west.

https://earthhow.com/weather-facts/

QUIZ ANSWERS
Weather Wonders

1. **B) Compression of air during the electrical discharge**

2. **C) Updrafts lift them repeatedly through different temperature zones**

3. **B) Air is pulled inward toward the approaching system**

4. **B) Lightning branches in many directions**

5. **B) Light bending twice inside raindrops**

6. **B) They lose warm ocean water as a fuel source**

7. **B) Light bending through layers of hot rising air**

FILL-IN-THE-BLANK ANSWERS

1. **petrichor**

2. **Sun**

3. **virga**

4. **bolt from the blue**

5. **jet stream**

6. **sun dogs**

7. **downburst**

3

WILDLIFE ENCOUNTERS

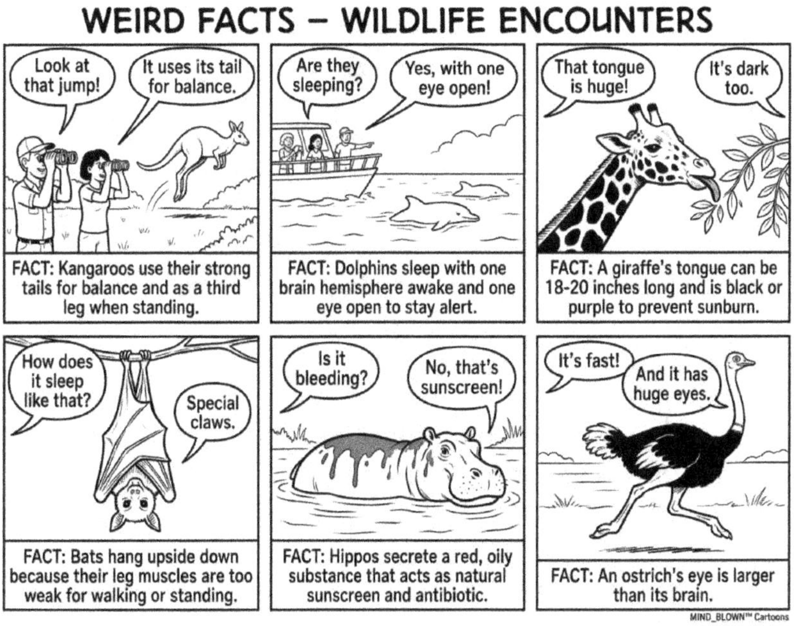

WEIRD & FUN FACTS
Wildlife Encounters

MIND-BLOWN MOMENT

- **A grizzly bear can smell food from over a mile away** because its nose contains **hundreds of millions** of scent receptors — far more than any dog.

- **A deer's eyes are on the sides of its head** to give it a **310-degree field of view**, letting it spot predators coming from almost any direction.

- **Owls fly almost silently** because the edges of their feathers have **tiny serrations** that break up the sound of airflow.

- **A beaver's teeth never stop growing**, so the animal must keep chewing wood to **file them down**.

- **Ravens can remember individual human faces** and will even **communicate danger** to other ravens about someone they distrust.

- **Mountain lions rarely roar** — they mostly hiss, chirp, or yowl because they lack the **special throat structure** that big "roaring cats" have.

- **Elk can bugle across long distances** because the sound bounces through a **long, flexible voice box** that amplifies the call.

- **Bison can run faster than a horse**, reaching **up to 35 mph**, despite weighing nearly a ton.

- **Bears aren't true hibernators** — they enter a **torpor**, a lighter sleep where they can wake quickly if threatened.

- 😎 **A coyote can hear a mouse moving under snow**, pinpointing the sound thanks to **high-frequency hearing**.

- 😎 **Bees communicate with a "waggle dance"** to show nestmates where to find nectar-rich flowers.

- 😎 **Some frogs freeze solid in winter** and thaw out in spring because their bodies produce **natural antifreeze**.

- 😎 **Porcupines don't shoot their quills**, but the quills detach easily because each one has **tiny backward-facing barbs**.

- 😎 **Moose are excellent swimmers**, moving comfortably through cold lakes thanks to **buoyant bodies** and long legs.

- 😎 **A wolf pack isn't led by an "alpha" in the Hollywood sense** — it's usually just a **mom and dad** leading their family.

- 😎 **Sharks can detect a drop of blood in an Olympic pool**, thanks to highly tuned **chemoreceptors**.

- 😎 **A squirrel's memory is so strong** it can retrieve nuts months later, guided by **smell, landmarks, and spatial mapping**.

- 😎 **Raccoons have incredibly sensitive paws** that can "see" textures because more than **two-thirds of their brain** is devoted to touch.

- 😎 **Giraffes barely sleep** — often just **20–30 minutes a day** in short naps.

- 😎 **Hyenas aren't primarily scavengers** — they hunt **far more animals** than lions do in many regions.

- 😎 **Platypuses produce venom** during the breeding season, delivered by **spurs on their back legs**.

- 😎 **A kangaroo can't hop backward** because of the **shape of its hips and tail**.

☻ **Bees can recognize human faces**, solving the same recognition task as primates but in a totally different way.

☻ **A cheetah's acceleration beats most sports cars** — it can reach 60 mph in about **three seconds**.

☻ **Some birds fake injury** to lure predators away from their nests, fluttering like they're hurt until the danger moves.

☻ **Turtles don't have vocal cords**, yet some species communicate through **low-frequency sounds**.

☻ **Foxes use the Earth's magnetic field** as a natural targeting system when pouncing on hidden prey.

☻ **Otters hold hands while sleeping** so they don't drift apart in the water.

☻ **Bees get tired**, and sometimes rest on flowers because their **energy drops** before they make it home.

☻ **A camel's humps store fat**, not water — the fat can be converted into **energy and moisture** during long droughts.

☻ **Orcas coordinate hunts** using sophisticated **vocal signals**, making them one of the most cooperative predators.

☻ **A woodpecker's skull acts like a helmet**, distributing shock so it doesn't injure its brain while pecking.

☻ **Deer can jump nearly eight feet high** thanks to powerful **hind leg muscles**.

☻ **Some spiders "balloon" through the air** by releasing silk that catches **electrostatic currents**, not just wind.

☻ **Coyotes and badgers sometimes hunt together**, combining speed above ground with digging ability below.

☻ **Bald eagles can lock their talons** and stay gripped even while asleep.

☻ **Lizards can drop their tails** to distract predators — the tail keeps moving because of **built-in nerve reflexes**.

☻ **Octopuses have three hearts**, pumping blood through **their entire soft body** to keep oxygen flowing.

☻ **Bats navigate with echolocation**, sending out tiny clicks and reading the echoes to build **a mental map** of their surroundings.

☻ **Some fish climb waterfalls**, using suction-cup-like fins to scale rock faces.

☻ **Horses can sleep standing up** because their legs contain a **locking mechanism** that prevents them from collapsing.

☻ **An eagle's eyesight is about eight times sharper than ours**, detecting movement a mile away.

WEIRD FACTS — WILDLIFE ENCOUNTERS

Those claws look serious...

Try 300 pounds of pressure.

FACT: Great horned owls can grip with enough force to crush bone.

Shouldn't it be worried?

It's immune to most of that venom.

FACT: Hedgehogs have cellular resistance to many snake venoms.

Wait... it's not actually white?

Its fur is transparent — it just reflects the snow.

FACT: Polar bear fur is clear, not white, reflecting surrounding light.

How is it still going?

"Wolves can run 30–40 miles a day."

FACT: Wolves are endurance runners built for long-distance travel.

"I can feel them from miles away."

FACT: Elephants detect underground vibrations from distant herds.

Did you hear something?"

"Nope, just leaves."

FACT: A sloth's slow movement and algae-covered fur make it nearly invisible to predators.

MIND-BLOWN™ Cartoons

MYTHS – BUSTED
Wildlife Encounters

Myth #1: "Bears can't run downhill."
Fact: They absolutely can — and very fast. Bears run on all fours with incredible balance, and their speed downhill can hit **35 mph**.

Myth #2: "If you see a baby animal alone, it's been abandoned."
Fact: Most mothers intentionally hide or leave young animals for hours at a time. They return quietly because **staying nearby attracts predators**.

Myth #3: "Snakes chase people."
Fact: They don't. What people think is "chasing" is usually a snake trying to escape to **the nearest cover**, which sometimes happens to be behind you.

Myth #4: "Porcupines can shoot their quills."
Fact: The quills detach **on contact**, but they don't fire from a distance. The myth came from animals backing into predators during panic.

Myth #5: "Deer freeze because they're confused."
Fact: They freeze because it's a defensive response called **"tonic immobility."** Staying still helps them avoid detection from predators that track movement.

Myth #6: "If a rabbit screams, it's faking to scare predators."
Fact: Rabbits scream only when terrified or injured. It's a **panic call**, not a trick.

Myth #7: "Coyotes hunt alone."
Fact: They often hunt **in pairs or small groups**, and will coordinate strategy, especially for large prey.

Myth #8: "Wolves howl at the moon."
Fact: Wolves howl to communicate, not because of the moon. They lift their heads to **project sound farther**, which makes it *look* like moon worship.

Myth #9: "Touching a toad gives you warts."
Fact: Warts are caused by **human viruses**, not toads. Toad skin bumps have nothing to do with the myth.

Myth #10: "A snake's tongue is dangerous."
Fact: The tongue is harmless. Snakes flick it to **collect scent particles**, not to attack.

WILD ENCOUNTERS

LEGENDS
Wildlife Encounters

LEGENDS

The Devil Bird of Sri Lanka

For generations, villagers described a nighttime shriek so human and horrifying it was believed to predict death. Hunters claimed it came from a huge, unseen bird with glowing eyes hiding in the canopy. Modern researchers eventually traced the scream to the spot-bellied eagle owl — one of the few birds whose call truly sounds like a dying person.

The Ghost Caribou of the Arctic

Inuit hunters speak of a herd that moves like smoke across the tundra — appearing suddenly, then vanishing without tracks or scent. Later explorers confirmed rare temperature-inversion mirages can make distant animals appear to float, shimmer, and disappear instantly as the air layers shift.

The Skinless Beast of the Orkneys

Old fishermen described a horse-shaped creature with no skin, red muscle exposed, dripping brine as it crawled from the surf. Many now believe the sightings came from storm-thrown seals suffering severe degloving injuries — a gruesome but real phenomenon that fed the legend's terror.

The Black Lion of Tsavo

Elders in eastern Kenya tell of a massive lion with a jet-black mane and eyes that glow without light. It appears before danger or hardship, then disappears. Rare, unusually dark-maned lions documented in the region — scarred and hardened by territorial battles — have kept the legend alive.

The Vanishing Puma of Patagonia

Shepherds insist a silent, ash-gray cat haunts the high plains, leaving no tracks and killing livestock without noise or drag marks. Biologists suspect a population of mountain lions adapted to volcanic ash flats, where tracks don't imprint — but the silence of the kills still unsettles locals.

The Thunderbird That Lifts Deer

Tribal accounts from across the Plains describe a monstrous bird that arrives with storms, its wings booming like thunder. Early frontier reports described giant birds seen after tempests, and some researchers believe these stories preserve memories of enormous, condor-like species that survived longer than science assumed.

MYTHS & LEGENDS

Ch3 — Wildlife Encounters

MIND-BLOWN™ Cartoons

DID YOU KNOW?
Wildlife Encounters

A bear's sense of smell is estimated to be seven times stronger than a bloodhound's, allowing it to detect food or carrion **from over a mile away**.

Crows can hold grudges, remembering specific human faces for years — and they **teach their young** who to avoid.

Beavers have transparent "third eyelids" that act like goggles underwater, letting them **see clearly while swimming**.

Owls don't have eyeballs — they have eye tubes, which is why their heads turn **almost 270 degrees** to make up for the lack of eye movement.

A mountain lion's scream can sound shockingly human, often mistaken for someone calling for help deep in the woods.

Hummingbirds can hover because they move their wings in a perfect figure-eight, giving them **lift on both the upstroke and downstroke**.

Snakes can "hear" through the ground, sensing vibrations through their **jawbones** even though they lack external ears.

Wolves can smell a carcass from several miles away, using wind direction like **a natural radar system**.

Some turtles can breathe through their rear ends, absorbing oxygen through **specialized tissue** when hibernating underwater.

Octopuses can solve puzzles and escape jars, showing a level of **problem-solving intelligence** rarely seen in invertebrates.

Raccoons can open latches, doors, and containers, thanks to their extremely sensitive and **dexterous front paws**.

A moose's long nose helps warm cold air before it reaches the lungs, acting like a **built-in heating system**.

Bald eagles sometimes steal fish mid-air from osprey, a behavior known as **piracy feeding**.

Squirrels will fake burying food to fool rivals watching them, a behavior known as **"deceptive caching."**

Porcupines are incredible climbers, helping them escape predators by retreating **straight up a tree**.

Sharks have special pores called ampullae of Lorenzini, which detect the **electrical fields** of living creatures.

Coyotes adapt their howls based on surroundings, using echoes to make small groups sound **much larger** than they are.

MIND-BLOWN Cartoons

What allows an owl to hear a mouse beneath a blanket of snow?
Their offset ears pick up tiny differences in sound timing.

Why do wolves howl in a way that sounds like multiple animals?
Their voices bounce off terrain and split into echoes.

What helps a snake follow an invisible scent trail across the forest floor?
Its tongue delivers particles to a special sensory organ.

How can raccoons "see" with their paws?
Most of their brain is devoted to touch instead of sight.

Why do deer raise their tails when alarmed?
The bright underside warns other deer of danger.

What allows a beaver to dive for long periods without coming up?
It slows its heartbeat to conserve oxygen.

How can a coyote hear rodents moving underground?
Its ears detect high-frequency sounds that humans can't hear.

Why do some birds dive-bomb hikers without warning?
They're defending hidden nests close to the ground.

Why does a lizard lose its tail. It is a survival technique. It normally grows back on many lizards..

Why do octopuses squeeze through holes smaller than your fist?
They have no bones holding them back.

What lets hawks track prey from hundreds of feet in the air?

Their vision is several times sharper than human eyesight.

Why do squirrels flick their tails when they spot danger?

It alerts nearby squirrels without making noise.

What makes a bear stand up on two legs?

Curiosity — it's trying to smell or see better, not act aggressively.

Why do some animals seem to vanish into the forest instantly?

Their fur patterns blend with moving shadows.

How can a bobcat move without making a sound?

Its padded feet muffle every step.

WEIRD FACTS — WILDLIFE ENCOUNTERS

Did... did it just jump?!

Three feet — straight up!

FACT: Startled armadillos can launch three feet straight upward — not ideal near highways.

Is it tasting the air?

Exactly — that's how snakes smell.

FACT: Snakes collect scent particles on their tongues and analyze them with a special organ.

It runs HOW fast?!

Thirty-five miles an hour. Don't race it.

FACT: A bear's top speed can hit 35 mph — much faster than most people imagine.

What's it following?

Rodent trails — they glow in ultraviolet.

FACT: Hawks can see ultraviolet, allowing them to track glowing rodent urine trails.

MIND-BLOWN™ Cartoons

STORY MOMENT
Wildlife Encounters

STORY MOMENT

There's a moment in the woods when everything shifts — a strange pause where the world seems to hold its breath. I was hiking a narrow ridge trail in the late afternoon, sunlight cutting sideways through the trees and turning the dust in the air into gold. I'd been listening to the usual forest soundtrack: wind in the branches, my pack straps creaking, a couple of jays arguing in the distance.

Then it all... stopped.

No breeze. No birds. Even the insects went silent. It was just the soft crunch of my boots and this sharp sense that something was watching me. And there he was — a large buck standing between two pines like he'd materialized there. Perfectly still. Calm in that ancient, wild way animals have when they know exactly where they belong.

He didn't flinch or spook. He just tilted his head slightly, sizing me up the way a local sizes up a tourist. For a few long seconds, we stood there in that quiet standoff.

Then, as if making some private decision, he stepped off the trail and slipped into the brush with impossible silence. And almost instantly, the forest turned its volume back on — wind returning, birds calling, life flowing like normal again.

Moments like that don't last long, but they stick with you. Years later, you can still feel that silence and that stare, reminding you that you're just a guest in a much bigger world.

QUIZ
Wildlife Encounters

QUIZ

QUIZ

Multiple Choice

1. What helps owls fly almost silently?
A. Hollow bones
B. Special serrated feathers
C. Slow wingbeats
D. Soft talons

2. Why do deer freeze when startled?
A. Their muscles lock
B. They're confused
C. It's an instinct to avoid movement-based predators
D. They can't see well at night

3. What allows bats to navigate in complete darkness?
A. Heat sensing
B. Night vision
C. Echolocation
D. Magnetic field detection

4. Why do raccoons "wash" their food?
A. To soften it
B. To remove dirt
C. To activate sensory nerves in their paws
D. To signal other raccoons

5. What makes a mountain lion's scream sound human?
A. Their vocal chords mimic speech
B. Air moving through a long throat structure

C. Echoes in the trees

D. They imitate prey

6. Why do wolves lift their heads when howling?

A. To look intimidating

B. To see stars

C. To project sound farther

D. To signal pups

7. What lets snakes "smell" with their tongues?

A. Sticky saliva

B. A special organ in the mouth

C. Heat-sensitive taste buds

D. Tongue pores

8. Why do some animals' eyes glow at night?

A. Moonlight reflection

B. Retinal dust

C. A reflective layer behind the retina

D. Large pupils

9. What allows squirrels to remember where they buried their food?

A. Scent markings

B. Magnetic fields

C. Their strong spatial memory

D. Following other squirrels

10. Why can beavers see underwater without blinking?

A. Built-in goggles

B. A transparent third eyelid

C. Special tear glands

D. Water-resistant eyelashes

Fill-in-the-Blank

1. Wolves communicate across long distances using powerful
_____.

2. Raccoons rely on extremely sensitive _____ to explore
objects.

3. A deer's wide field of view comes from its eyes being placed on
the _____ of its head.

4. Owls can rotate their heads nearly 270 degrees because they
have more _____ in their necks.

5. Snakes analyze scent particles using the _____ organ.

6. Beavers slap their _____ on water as a warning signal.

7. Flying squirrels glide using a flap of skin called a _____.

8. Moose use their long _____ to warm cold air before it
reaches their lungs.

9. A wolf pack is usually led by the breeding pair, often called the
_____ pair.

10. Octopuses navigate tight spaces easily because they lack a rigid
_____.

QUIZ ANSWERS
Wildlife Encounters

Multiple Choice Answers

1. **B** — Special serrated feathers
2. **C** — It's an instinct to avoid movement-based predators
3. **C** — Echolocation
4. **C** — To activate sensory nerves in their paws
5. **B** — Air moving through a long throat structure
6. **C** — To project sound farther
7. **B** — A special organ in the mouth
8. **C** — A reflective layer behind the retina
9. **C** — Their strong spatial memory
10. **B** — A transparent third eyelid

Fill-in-the-Blank Answers

1. **Howls**
2. **Paws**
3. **Sides**
4. **Extra vertebrae**
5. **Jacobson's** (or **Vomeronasal**) organ
6. **Tails**
7. **Patagium**
8. **Nose**
9. **Breeding** pair
10. **Skeleton** (or **bones**)

4

OUTDOOR SURVIVAL

'WEIRD FACTS'

'Ch4 — Outdoor Survival'   MIND-BLOWN™ Cartoons

WEIRD & FUN FACTS
OUTDOOR SURVIVAL

MIND-BLOWN
MOMENT

⚡ **You can survive weeks without food but only about three days without water**, because your body needs water to regulate temperature and keep organs working.

⚡ **Clear, running water isn't guaranteed safe** — fast-moving streams can still carry **parasites** that cause serious illness.

⚡ **The human body loses heat 25 times faster in water** because water pulls heat away much more efficiently than air.

⚡ **You can start a fire with steel wool and a battery** — the fibers spark instantly when they touch both battery terminals.

⚡ **In cold weather, most heat loss happens from lack of insulation**, not from your head, despite the old myth.

⚡ **Rubbing two sticks together only works with the right wood pairings**, because certain woods generate the **friction and dust** needed for an ember.

⚡ **Most wild berries are not safe to eat**, and bright colors often signal **toxicity**, not nutrition.

⚡ **Carrying a whistle is more effective than shouting** because its high pitch travels farther and uses far less energy.

⚡ **You can navigate using the sun's shadow** by marking its position every 15 minutes — the line you draw points **east–west**.

⚡ **Cactus water is mostly unsafe to drink**, causing vomiting or dehydration because many cacti contain **toxic alkaloids**.

⚡ **Your sense of direction gets worse when you're tired**, and people naturally walk in circles unless using a visual reference.

⚡ **Most snakes strike only when threatened**, and vibration from footsteps usually warns them long before you get close.

⚡ **Dry grass and leaves can ignite from a single spark**, especially in low humidity where fuels lose moisture quickly.

⚡ **Carrying too much gear tires you faster than walking longer distances**, because excessive weight increases heat production.

⚡ **The color of your clothing affects insect attraction**, with dark colors drawing mosquitoes more than light ones.

⚡ **A simple bandana can serve as a pre-filter** for muddy water, removing sediment before purification.

⚡ **Hypothermia can happen in temperatures above 50°F** when you're wet, tired, or exposed to wind, because the body cools rapidly under those conditions.

⚡ **The smell of smoke carries incredibly far**, allowing lost hikers to signal others without shouting.

⚡ **Sitting still when lost helps rescuers find you faster**, because people who keep wandering create a larger search area.

⚡ **Fresh animal tracks can clue you in to nearby water**, since animals often follow repeated routes to **reliable sources**.

⚡ **Dehydration often feels like hunger**, causing people to eat instead of drink, which worsens water loss.

⚡ **Carrying a small mirror or reflective object can act as an emergency signal**, flashing sunlight miles away.

⚡ **Humans can hear running water long before they see it**, giving a natural clue toward possible water sources.

⚡ **Duct tape can patch torn gear, seal wounds briefly, or protect blisters**, making it one of the most versatile survival tools.

⚡ **Smoke from green leaves creates thicker, darker plumes**, which stand out better for signaling.

⚡ **A fire's color reveals how well it's burning** — blue or white flames mean **hot and clean**, while orange means **cooler and sootier**.

⚡ **Eating snow drops core body temperature** and increases dehydration, because melting it takes energy and heat.

⚡ **A sudden silence in the woods often means a predator or large animal is nearby**, as smaller creatures freeze or flee.

⚡ **Bird paths can reveal direction**, since many species follow consistent **morning and evening routes**.

⚡ **If you find moss only on one side of trees, it usually means there's a slope**, not a compass direction.

⚡ **You can judge daylight left by stacking fingers below the sun**, estimating minutes per "finger" based on height.

⚡ **Wind direction changes ahead of storms**, giving an early clue about shifting weather.

⚡ **Carrying two light sources prevents panic**, since losing your only flashlight causes disorientation in darkness.

⚡ **Fires made with resin-rich woods like pine ignite quickly**, because resin burns hotter and longer.

⚡ **In survival situations, the biggest threat is often panic**, not the environment.

⚡ **If your feet get wet, drying them quickly prevents blisters**, since moisture softens skin.

⚡ **Climbing a hill doesn't always improve your view**, because forest canopy can block visibility more than low terrain.

⚡ **Bears rarely attack humans,** and most encounters end with the bear retreating unless it feels cornered.

⚡ **Ferns often grow in moist areas**, offering clues about hidden springs or seepages.

You can predict weather from cloud movement, since faster clouds often signal **approaching fronts**.

If you smell rain before seeing clouds, humidity may be rising rapidly ahead of a storm.

A sudden drop in temperature at sunset increases dew formation, which can help you collect moisture on surfaces.

Tree bark patterns can reveal wind exposure, as harsh winds sculpt one side more than the other.

Shelter is more important than fire in cold, wet weather, because staying dry protects core temperature.

Following animal trails can lead to water, but they can also lead to predators — always observe before committing.

Your ears adjust faster than your eyes in the dark, giving an early warning of movement before you see anything.

Some plants grow in straight "bands" along slopes, marking changes in soil moisture or sunlight.

A simple tarp shelter blocks more wind than you'd expect, especially when angled correctly.

Metal tools and knives are most effective when dry, since moisture weakens grip and accuracy.

WEIRD FACTS — OUTDOOR SURVIVAL

MIND-BLOWN™ Cartoons

MYTHS – BUSTED
OUTDOOR SURVIVAL

MYTHS

Myth #1: "Moss grows only on the north side of trees."
Fact: Moss grows where it's **moist**, not where the compass points. Shade patterns and humidity matter more than direction.

Myth #2: "You can drink water from any running stream."
Fact: Moving water can still contain **parasites** like giardia — always filter or boil it.

Myth #3: "Eating snow is fine in winter emergencies."
Fact: It lowers your core temperature and speeds **dehydration** unless melted first.

Myth #4: "You'll scare off predators by yelling."
Fact: Noise helps, but some animals interpret yelling as **threat behavior**, which can escalate danger.

Myth #5: "A big fire keeps all wildlife away."
Fact: Some animals are **attracted** to firelight out of curiosity or to hunt insects drawn by the glow.

Myth #6: "Carrying a knife is the most important survival tool."
Fact: Knowledge beats gear. A knife helps, but skills like **navigation, shelter-building, and calm decision-making** matter far more.

Myth #7: "If you're lost, follow the nearest animal trail."
Fact: Some trails lead to water, but many lead to **feeding grounds or dens**, not safe human routes.

Myth #8: "You can suck venom from a snakebite."
Fact: This method doesn't work and may worsen tissue damage.
The real key is **staying calm, immobilizing the limb** .

Myth #9: "If you touch poison ivy once, you're immune next time."
Fact: Sensitivity increases with exposure — reactions can get **worse**, not better.

Myth #10: "You can always make fire by rubbing sticks together."
Fact: It requires **specific woods, perfect dryness, and technique** — it's not reliable for real emergencies.

MYTHS & LEGENDS

LEGENDS
OUTDOOR SURVIVAL

LEGENDS

The Lost Cabin of the Superstition Mountains

For more than a century, prospectors in Arizona insisted a lone miner discovered a hidden gold vein and built a small cabin beside it. According to the legend, anyone who tried to follow his hand-drawn directions found the landmarks "shifting," ridge lines changing shape, and trails that seemed to rearrange themselves. Early survey teams said the desert heat, dehydration, and maze-like terrain created the illusion of moving geography — but the story still keeps hikers alert in the Superstitions.

The Wendigo Winter Trails

Northern tribes and frontier trappers told of a gaunt winter spirit that left long, single-file tracks across frozen lakes and deep forest snow. Early explorers wrote about the same strange prints: too long for a person, too narrow for a moose, and disappearing without explanation. The real cause was a snow phenomenon called "snow splay," where drifting powder collapses into stretched shapes overnight. Still, the legend lingered because the tracks always appeared during the hungriest, coldest months of winter.

The Phantom Drummer of the Maine Woods

Lumber crews in the 1800s claimed they heard slow, rhythmic drumming echo through the pine forests — steady beats with no visible source. Search parties found nothing, and the sound often stopped the moment anyone moved closer. Naturalists eventually identified the cause: wind flowing across hollow stumps and fallen

64

logs, producing deep pulses that bounced across the valley floor. Even today, old logging families say the "drummer" still warns woodsmen when bad weather is coming.

The Disappearing Lake of Yellowstone

Early explorers described a small mountain lake that seemed to vanish each spring — full one week, gone the next, leaving cracked mud and stunned fish behind. It sounded supernatural until geologists discovered hidden sinkholes under the basin. When snowmelt arrived, entire pools of water drained straight into underground channels, as if someone pulled a giant plug. Visitors still call it the place "where water packs up and leaves."

The Crying Rocks of the Blue Ridge

Hikers in the Blue Ridge Mountains have long reported hearing soft wails or sobbing near certain rock faces at night. Early settlers believed lost spirits haunted the ridges, and modern campers say the sound can still freeze you in place. Scientists later found that water trapped in rock fractures expands or contracts with temperature shifts, forcing air through tiny openings and producing eerie, voice-like tones. On cold nights, the stones truly "cry," and the legend endures because the sound sticks with you.

The Ghost Fire

Campers swore a campfire once lit itself in an empty clearing — no people, no footsteps, just flames flickering in the dark. A few even claimed the fire "sighed" before it died out. The real cause was far less supernatural: old embers buried under dry leaves were stirred back to life by a sudden late-night wind. The leaves ignited just long enough to flare, breathe, and collapse, creating the eerie illusion of a fire that woke up on its own.

The Silent Forest of Aokigahara (Japan)

For centuries, travelers near Mount Fuji spoke of a forest so quiet that even footsteps seemed swallowed by the trees. Early explorers believed spirits muted the air, but the real cause is volcanic soil and dense, twisted growth that absorbs sound unusually well. The silence is so complete that many hikers report feeling disoriented, as if the forest itself is closing in around them.

The Lights of Min Min (Australia)

Outback ranchers and night travelers have long reported glowing balls of light drifting across the plains. These Min Min lights hover, retreat when approached, or glide silently above the scrub. Scientists point to atmospheric refraction bending distant light sources or heat-inversion layers creating mirages, while others note bioluminescent insects. The phenomenon is still seen today, keeping the legend alive in the outback.

The Singing Dunes of Kazakhstan

For generations, desert travelers described dunes that produced deep, booming notes when the sand shifted — like a massive, low-pitched musical instrument. Ancient groups believed spirits lived beneath the dunes. Modern researchers discovered that perfectly dry, uniform sand grains can create powerful resonant frequencies when they slide, causing entire hillsides to "sing" or rumble in eerie tones.

DID YOU KNOW? OUTDOOR SURVIVAL

Why does your sense of direction get worse when you're tired?
Fatigue affects memory and decision-making, making landmarks harder to recall.

How can birds help you find water?
They often fly **morning and evening routes** between roosting and drinking spots.

Why do anxious hikers feel like they're being watched?
The brain becomes hyper-alert under stress, misinterpreting **normal sounds**.

What makes a small shelter warmer than a big one?
Less space means your body heat **traps faster**, raising the temperature.

Why do some people panic when darkness falls?
Lack of visual anchors increases **disorientation**, especially in dense forests.

How can fires signal rescuers more effectively?
Adding green leaves creates **dark, thick smoke** that stands out against sky.

Why does damp clothing feel colder than wet skin alone?
Cloth holds **moving air**, accelerating heat loss.

How can rocks give clues to direction?
One side often grows **more lichen** depending on shade and moisture.

Why do footsteps sound louder at night?
Cool, dense air carries **sound more efficiently** after sunset.

How can you estimate the time left before sunset without a watch?
Stacking fingers under the sun gives a <u>rough</u> count of **minutes per finger**.

Did you know that your sense of smell gets sharper when you're lost?
When the brain switches into "threat assessment" mode, scent-processing speeds up, helping you detect water, smoke, or animals you normally wouldn't notice.

Did you know moss doesn't always grow on the north side of trees?
It grows where **shade and moisture** persist the longest — which might be north, but could also be east or even near root cavities. You need multiple tree checks, not just one.

Did you know your breath can reveal incoming weather?
If your breath suddenly becomes visible at the same temperature, rising humidity is often the cause — a hint that fog or precipitation may be forming soon.

Did you know the forest "quieting down" can signal nearby wildlife?
Birds and small mammals freeze or go silent when large animals move through, creating an eerie hush that experienced hikers listen for.

"WEIRD FACTS!"

Ch3 — Wildlife Encounters

MIND-BLOWN™ Cartoons

69

STORY MOMENT
OUTDOOR SURVIVAL

STORY MOMENT

I once wandered off a main trail during an early fall hike — nothing dramatic, just one of those "this side path looks interesting" choices. It started out wide and well-traveled, then squeezed into a tight tunnel of brush before I realized, *yeah... this isn't a real trail.* The trees looked different, the air felt heavier, and that subtle sense of **uh-oh** hit fast.

For a moment, the stubborn voice in my head said, *Just keep going.* But that's how people turn a minor detour into a rescue story, so I stopped. Completely. No pushing forward. No panic. Just a full reset.

I shut up, listened, and let the woods talk. Behind the wind and distant bird calls, I caught a steady sound — running water. That became my anchor. Streams don't lie, and they usually run near real trails. I aimed toward the sound, clicked on my flashlight, and backed out the way I came, keeping my eyes in the direction I'd entered.

It took longer than expected, and there were a couple moments where the dark closed in, but then the ground felt more packed and the space opened up. A few steps later, I stepped back onto the main trail like I'd just been spit out by the forest. Instant relief.

Survival isn't always dramatic. Most of the time, it's the quiet decision to **stop, breathe, assess, and backtrack** before ego pulls you deeper into trouble. And ever since that day, every "shortcut" gets a second look.

QUIZ
OUTDOOR SURVIVAL

QUIZ

Multiple Choice

1. What's the most important priority in most survival situations?
A. Finding food
B. Building shelter
C. Getting rescued
D. Starting a fire

2. Why is boiling water the safest purification method?
A. It softens minerals
B. It removes dirt
C. It kills pathogens
D. It improves taste

3. What's the biggest danger of eating snow?
A. Too much sodium
B. It cools your core temperature
C. It's dirty
D. It melts too slowly

4. Why is sitting still helpful when you realize you're lost?
A. It calms animals
B. It conserves energy and reduces panic
C. It cools your body
D. It helps you fall asleep

5. What makes a whistle better than yelling for help?
A. It's quieter
B. It uses less energy and carries farther
C. It scares animals
D. It confuses predators

71

6. Why do small shelters stay warmer than big ones?

A. They trap body heat better
B. They block bugs
C. They make fire easier
D. They reflect sunlight

7. What's the biggest danger of following animal trails?

A. They're noisy
B. They often lead to predator areas
C. They're too muddy
D. They're too straight

8. Why is wet clothing dangerous in cold weather?

A. It smells bad
B. It attracts insects
C. It increases heat loss
D. It blocks sunlight

9. What's the biggest threat in survival situations?

A. Running
B. Panic
C. Eating too little
D. Carrying gear

10. Why is dark smoke better for signaling?

A. It looks cooler
B. It rises slower
C. It contrasts strongly with the sky
D. It smells stronger

Fill-in-the-Blank

1. You can purify water by _____ it for one full minute.

2. A simple _____ can act as a powerful emergency signal when reflecting sunlight.

3. Eating snow increases _____, not hydration.

4. A small, steady fire produces more usable heat than a large, _____ one.

5. Lost hikers should pause, breathe, and avoid _____ decisions.

True or False

1. Moss reliably shows you which way is north.
2. You should always yell loudly to scare off wildlife.
3. Darkness increases disorientation because visual cues disappear.

WEIRD FACTS

Moss doesn't always grow on the north side of trees.
Don't use me as a compass.

You can start a fire with a water bottle on a sunny day.
Magnify the chaos.
We feel the pressure drop.

Certain ants can predict approaching storms.
We feel the pressure drop.

Eating snow lowers your core temperature fast.
Don't slurp me.

Birch bark burns even when wet.
Nature built me flammable.

You can tell direction by watching how trees lean.
Wind leaves clues.

Ch4 — Outdoor Survival

MIND-BLOWN™ Cartoons

QUIZ ANSWERS
OUTDOOR SURVIVAL

Multiple Choice Answers

1. **C** — Getting rescued
2. **C** — It kills pathogens
3. **B** — It cools your core temperature
4. **B** — It conserves energy and reduces panic
5. **B** — It uses less energy and carries farther
6. **A** — They trap body heat better
7. **B** — They often lead to predator areas
8. **C** — It increases heat loss
9. **B** — Panic
10. C — It contrasts strongly with the sky

Fill-in-the-Blank Answers

1. Boiling
2. Mirror
3. Dehydration
4. Smoky
5. Panic-driven (or simply panic)

True or False Answers

1. False
2. False
3. True

5

NIGHT SKY

Ch5 — Night Sky

WEIRD & FUN FACTS
NIGHT SKY

MIND-BLOWN
MOMENT

✦ **The Milky Way you see overhead is only a tiny slice of our galaxy,** which contains hundreds of billions of stars that stretch far beyond what the eye can see.

✦ **Your eyes need about 20–30 minutes to fully adjust to darkness,** and during that time your ability to see faint stars improves dramatically.

✦ **Starlight you see tonight may be hundreds or thousands of years old,** because light takes time to travel across space.

✦ **Sirius is the brightest star in the sky,** not because it's huge, but because it's **close and intensely luminous**.

✦ **The color of a star tells you its temperature,** with blue stars being hotter than red ones.

✦ **You can sometimes see satellites move across the sky,** traveling in steady, silent lines that don't blink like aircraft lights.

✦ **Shooting stars are tiny pieces of space dust,** burning up at thousands of degrees as they hit Earth's atmosphere.

✦ **A full moon can be bright enough to cast shadows,** especially in snow-covered landscapes.

✦ **The North Star (Polaris) isn't perfectly aligned with true north,** but it's close enough to navigate with.

✦ **Venus is often mistaken for a UFO,** because it shines brighter than almost anything else in the sky.

✦ **The Sun is technically a yellow dwarf**, which is smaller and cooler than many of the massive blue or red stars out there.

✦ **The Moon is slowly drifting away from Earth**, moving about an inch and a half farther every year.

✦ **Planets shine steadily while stars twinkle**, because planets' light travels through less atmospheric distortion.

✦ **The sky appears blue during the day because of Rayleigh scattering**, which bends shorter blue wavelengths more than other colors.

✦ **The faint band of the Milky Way is brighter in the summer**, because we're facing the galaxy's core.

✦ **No two constellations are actually close together**, even though they look connected from Earth's perspective.

✦ **Earth's rotation makes the stars appear to move**, completing a full sky rotation every 23 hours and 56 minutes.

✦ **Meteor showers happen when Earth passes through old comet trails**, filled with leftover dust and debris.

✦ **If the Moon looks huge on the horizon, it's an optical illusion**, not actual size change.

✦ **Orion is one of the few constellations visible from both hemispheres**, thanks to its position along the celestial equator.

✦ **Cold nights offer clearer skies**, because cool air holds less moisture and dust.

✦ **Older cultures used the sky as a calendar**, tracking movements of stars to guide planting seasons and migrations.

✦ **The Big Dipper isn't a constellation**, but part of a larger constellation called **Ursa Major**.

✦ **Red lights are used by astronomers** because they preserve night vision better than white light.

✦ **Space is completely silent**, because sound waves can't travel in a vacuum.

✦ **Many stars you see with the naked eye are actually binary systems**, two stars orbiting each other.

✦ **The Moon's "man in the moon" face is made from ancient lava flows**, called maria, that hardened billions of years ago.

✦ **Even with perfect eyes, you can only see about 2,500 stars at once**, and that's in ideal darkness.

✦ **The Milky Way has a supermassive black hole at its center**, millions of times heavier than the Sun.

✦ **Comets have two tails**, one made of dust and one made of gas.

✦ **The night sky looks different throughout the year**, because Earth orbits the Sun and faces different regions of space.

✦ **The ISS circles Earth about every 90 minutes**, making it one of the fastest-moving objects you'll ever see.

✦ **Mars appears red due to iron oxide — essentially rust**, covering its surface.

✦ **A "blue moon" isn't actually blue**, it just means the second full moon in a single month.

✦ **Stars in the southern hemisphere are completely different**, and constellations like the Southern Cross never appear up north.

✦ **Your shadow at night can come from Jupiter or Venus**, when conditions are dark enough.

✦ **A completely dark, moonless sky is so rare** that most people never experience it without traveling far from cities.

✦ **Ancient sailors navigated entire oceans by starlight**, using the sky as their map long before compasses existed.

✦ **Space isn't cold — it has no temperature**, but objects in space can get extremely hot or cold depending on sunlight.

✦ **Nebulas are gigantic clouds of gas**, some so large they could hold thousands of solar systems.

✦ **A day on Venus is longer than a year on Venus**, because the planet rotates extremely slowly.

✦ **The Moon's gravity stabilizes Earth's tilt**, helping maintain seasons and long-term climate.

✦ **Jupiter acts like a giant shield**, its gravity pulling in asteroids that might otherwise hit Earth.

✦ **The stars in a constellation aren't permanent**, and over thousands of years they drift into new shapes.

✦ **Solar storms can cause the northern lights**, as charged particles collide with atoms high in Earth's atmosphere.

✦ **Looking at a bright phone screen erases your night vision instantly,** forcing your eyes to readjust for another 20 minutes.

✦ **Most constellations came from ancient Greek, Roman, and Middle Eastern storytelling**, passed down for centuries.

✦ **If you see a bright streak with a long tail, it may be a bolide**, a rare meteor that explodes in the atmosphere.

✦ **Dark-sky parks exist to protect natural night skies**, shielding them from artificial light pollution.

✦ **Mars can appear larger every 26 months**, during its close approach to Earth.

✦ **Saturn's rings are made of ice chunks**, ranging from tiny grains to pieces the size of houses.

✦ **Light pollution makes the Milky Way invisible to 80% of people**, even though it should be bright overhead.

WEIRD FACTS!

"The Milky Way is so wide that its light takes 100,000 years to cross from one side to the other."

"Some stars spin so fast they bulge like squashed pumpkins."

"Venus is bright enough to cast shadows on a clear night."

"Space telescopes can see galaxies whose light left before humans even existed."

"The moon once had an active magnetic field strong enough to affect early Earth."

"Some meteors explode so brightly they're called fireballs—you can see them even behind thin clouds."

Ch5 — Night Sky

MIND-BLOWN™ Cartoons

80

MYTHS – BUSTED
NIGHT SKY

Myth #1: "The Moon glows on its own."
Fact: The Moon shines by reflecting **sunlight**, not from emitting light.

Myth #2: "Stars twinkle because they're moving."
Fact: Twinkling happens because Earth's **atmosphere bends light**, not because stars wiggle in space.

Myth #3: "The Big Dipper is a constellation."
Fact: It's just part of a constellation — the full figure is **Ursa Major**, the Great Bear.

Myth #4: "The Milky Way is a cloud."
Fact: That milky streak is the **dense central band** of our galaxy.

Myth #5: "Shooting stars are real stars."
Fact: They're **tiny bits of dust** burning up in the atmosphere.

Myth #6: "The Moon's phases come from Earth's shadow."
Fact: Phases are created by the **Moon's angle to the Sun**, not by eclipses.

Myth #7: "All planets look the same in the sky."
Fact: Each planet has its own **brightness, color, and motion**, making them surprisingly easy to identify.

Myth #8: "Full moons cause more strange behavior."
Fact: Studies show no consistent effect — the full Moon's main power is casting **brighter light**, not causing chaos.

LEGENDS
NIGHT SKY

LEGENDS

The Wandering Star of the Polynesian Navigators

For hundreds of years, Polynesian sailors spoke of a "wandering star" that guided them across the Pacific. It wasn't a myth at all — they were tracking Venus, which changes position dramatically throughout the year. To early navigators, it appeared to drift across the sky like a living guide, earning a reputation as the star that "walks before the canoe."

The Aurora Wolves of the Inuit

Inuit communities told of glowing, shifting lights in the sky created by the spirits of wolves racing across the heavens. The lights would shimmer, pulse, and chase each other like running animals. The real phenomenon, of course, is the aurora borealis — charged particles hitting Earth's magnetic field — but the wolf legend became one of the most enduring interpretations of the northern lights.

The Seven Sisters Who Fled into the Sky

Across cultures from Greece to Indigenous Australia, there are legends about seven sisters chased across the earth by a persistent hunter until they escaped into the sky. Astronomers later noted these stories all describe the Pleiades star cluster — one of the few clusters visible to the naked eye. The matching stories across unrelated cultures fascinated early anthropologists because the myth is older than recorded history.

The Milky Way as the "Path of Spirits"

Early Native American tribes believed the Milky Way was a glowing road that the spirits of the dead walked on their journey to the afterlife. The long, hazy band of stars stretching across the sky was unmistakable at night in the pre-electric world. Different tribes had different variations, but the idea of a "sky path" appears in many cultures long before astronomy explained it as billions of distant stars.

The "Blood Moon" Warnings of Ancient Mesopotamia

Ancient Mesopotamian astronomers viewed lunar eclipses — when the moon turns dark red — as dangerous omens tied to the fate of kings. They kept detailed eclipse records on clay tablets and sometimes appointed a temporary "substitute king" to absorb any bad cosmic luck. Modern science shows the red color is simply sunlight filtered through Earth's atmosphere, but the eclipse legends were among the earliest attempts to predict sky events.

MYTHS & LEGENDS — NIGHT SKY WONDERS

That's Orion the Hunter! / He looks like he's fighting!
FACT: The stars of Orion are at vastly different distances from Earth.

The Seven Sisters! / Why only see six?
FACT: Only six Pleiades stars are easily visible; the seventh is faint.

A road of milk? / Legend says it's a path.
FACT: The Milky Way is a galaxy of billions of stars, not a fluid.

Is that a big bear? / "Looks like a ladle."
FACT: The Big Dipper is an asterism within the larger constellation Ursa Major, the Great Bear.

Spirits dancing? / "Ancestors' souls."
FACT: Auroras are caused by solar particles interacting with Earth's magnetic field.

A bad omen? / "A sign of change."
FACT: Comets are icy bodies from the outer solar system, not signs of doom.

MIND-BLOWN™ Cartoons

DID YOU KNOW? NIGHT SKY

What causes the northern lights?
Charged solar particles colliding with atoms high in the atmosphere.

Why do planets shine steadily while stars flicker?
Planets' light travels through **less atmospheric distortion**.

What makes Venus the brightest object in the night sky besides the Moon?
Its **reflective cloud layer** and its closeness to Earth.

How long does it take your eyes to adjust to darkness?
About **20–30 minutes**.

Why do stars appear to move across the sky?
Because **Earth rotates**, making them appear to slide overhead.

Did you know the Milky Way is only visible from truly dark places?
Light pollution washes it out, so most people today never see the galaxy they live in with the naked eye.

Did you know shooting stars aren't stars at all?
They're tiny pieces of dust or rock burning up in Earth's atmosphere at tens of thousands of miles per hour.

Did you know the Moon looks bigger near the horizon for psychological reasons, not physical ones?
Your brain compares it to trees and buildings, making it appear larger even though its actual size in the sky never changes.

STORY MOMENT
NIGHT SKY

STORY
MOMENT

I once camped in a wide, lonely meadow miles from the nearest road — the kind of place where the silence has weight and even your breathing feels loud. After the fire settled into a red glow and the last sparks threaded into the dark, the sky opened like someone had pulled a curtain. Stars didn't just appear — they *poured* across the black. The Milky Way stretched overhead in a bright, ghostly band, and far on the horizon a soft orange bloom marked a town so distant it felt like part of another world.

I stretched out on the cold grass, letting my eyes adjust, and the longer I looked, the more the night revealed its layers. Satellites drifted like slow-moving needles of light. A faint green tint shimmered low to the north — not enough to call an aurora, but enough to make you wonder. Somewhere far off, an owl called once and then went silent, as if the sky itself had asked for quiet.

Then it happened — a sharp, brilliant streak tore across the darkness, bright enough that the meadow flashed pale for half a heartbeat. It arced, flared, and burned out in a clean, silent fade that left the world feeling strangely suspended.

Everything stopped. No wind. No insects. Not even the subtle rustle of the grass. Just the massive, calm ceiling of stars looking down like they'd been waiting for someone to notice them.

Out there, under all that quiet, you remember things you forget in regular life — that the world is bigger than whatever you're wrestling with, older than the noise we drown in, and steadier than the stress we drag around. The night sky doesn't lecture you. It just shows you the truth from a few million miles away and lets you sit with it.

? QUIZ
NIGHT SKY

QUIZ

Multiple Choice

1. Why do stars twinkle?
A. They move rapidly
B. Light bends through Earth's atmosphere
C. They flicker on and off
D. They spin quickly

2. What makes the Milky Way visible?
A. Cloud reflection
B. Sunlight
C. Dense collections of distant stars
D. Moonlight

3. Which planet is usually the brightest in the sky?
A. Mars
B. Saturn
C. Jupiter
D. Venus

4. What causes shooting stars?
A. Exploding planets
B. Fired spacecraft
C. Dust burning in the atmosphere
D. Clouds splitting

5. Why does the Moon appear huge on the horizon?
A. It gets closer
B. Optical illusion

C. More sunlight
D. Air magnification

6. Why do astronomers use red lights?
A. Red light looks cool
B. Red preserves night vision
C. Red scares wildlife
D. Red reflects starlight better

7. How long does it take for full night vision?
A. 1 minute
B. 5 minutes
C. 30 minutes
D. 2 hours

8. What does Mars look like?
A. Blue
B. Purple
C. Red
D. Silver

9. Why do constellations change shape over thousands of years?
A. Stars burn out
B. Stars drift through space
C. Atmosphere thickens
D. Earth slows down

10. Why are dark-sky parks important?
A. They protect wildlife
B. They reduce wind
C. They protect natural night skies from light pollution
D. They make stars brighter

QUIZ ANSWERS
NIGHT SKY

Multiple Choice

1. **B** — Light bends through Earth's atmosphere

2. **C** — Dense collections of distant stars

3. **D** — Venus

4. **C** — Dust burning in the atmosphere

5. **B** — Optical illusion

6. **B** — Red preserves night vision

7. **C** — 30 minutes

8. **C** — Red

9. **B** — Stars drift through space

10. **C** — They protect natural night skies

6

RIVERS, LAKES & WATER

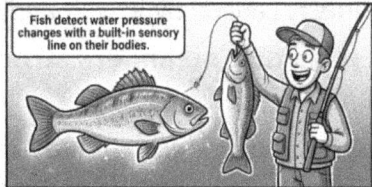

WEIRD & FUN FACTS
RIVERS, LAKES & WATER

MIND-BLOWN MOMENT

≋ **Freshwater makes up only about 2.5% of Earth's water,** and most of it is locked in glaciers or underground.

≋ **Rivers don't flow because they're "pushed" — they move because gravity constantly pulls water downhill,** even when the slope looks flat.

≋ **A river's speed changes hour by hour,** depending on rain, temperature, and snowmelt upstream.

≋ **The Amazon River carries more water than the next seven largest rivers combined,** making it the most powerful river system on Earth.

≋ **Lake Baikal in Russia holds more freshwater than all the Great Lakes combined,** thanks to its extreme depth.

≋ **Water looks blue in deep lakes because it absorbs red light first,** leaving only shorter blue wavelengths visible.

≋ **Most lakes are less than 12,000 years old,** created after the last Ice Age carved basins in the land.

≋ **You can sometimes hear lakes "sing" or "whistle" in winter,** caused by ice expanding and cracking under pressure.

≋ **A river that meanders strongly is actually slowing down,** depositing sediment on inner bends and eroding outer bends.

≋ **Animals use rivers as natural highways,** following them for migration, feeding, and shelter.

≋ **Lake-effect snow happens because cold air passing over warmer water picks up moisture,** creating intense snowfall downwind.

≋ **Water can carve solid rock**, given enough time, pressure, and sediment.

≋ **Clear water isn't always safe to drink**, because parasites and microscopic organisms may still be present.

≋ **Human bodies float more easily in cold freshwater**, because cold water is denser and increases buoyancy.

≋ **Some rivers disappear underground**, traveling through limestone caves and re-emerging miles away.

≋ **Rip currents form in lakes as well as oceans**, especially near piers and jetties.

≋ **The color of a river can reveal its health**, with green suggesting algae-rich water and brown indicating suspended sediment.

≋ **Many fish rely on polarized light to navigate**, something humans can only see with special lenses.

≋ **Lakes can flip over in a process called turnover**, when surface and deep waters exchange positions due to temperature changes.

≋ **A small creek can become dangerous within minutes** during flash floods, rising faster than most people expect.

≋ **Rivers naturally want to straighten over time**, cutting through bends and forming oxbow lakes.

≋ **Lake levels can rise from strong winds**, piling water against one shore in a process called a **seiche**.

≋ **Some rivers run "backwards" temporarily during storms**, when wind or floods push water upstream.

≋ **The Mississippi River once flowed in reverse for several hours** after a major earthquake in 1812.

≋ **Floating logs can travel thousands of miles**, guided by currents, storms, and seasonal floods.

≋ **Freshwater jellyfish exist**, though they're tiny and harmless.

≋ **Water temperature controls fish movement**, with many species avoiding sudden cold drops.

≋ **A wide river is usually shallower than a narrow one**, because water spreads out when it has room.

≋ **Many lakes formed from meteor impacts**, leaving deep, round basins.

≋ **Some lakes stay frozen nine months of the year**, creating unique ecosystems beneath the ice.

≋ **Rivers carry nutrients that feed entire forests**, spreading life far beyond the water's edge.

≋ **You can estimate direction using riverbanks**, as erosion typically happens on the **outer curves**.

≋ **Most river deltas are shrinking**, due to dams blocking sediment and rising sea levels.

≋ **Beavers transform entire water systems**, slowing rivers, creating ponds, and improving biodiversity.

≋ **Cold water shock is more dangerous than drowning**, because it disrupts breathing and muscle control immediately.

≋ **Some lakes have layers that never mix**, trapping ancient water at the bottom.

≋ **Lightning striking a lake sends current across the surface**, not deep underwater.

≋ **The Great Lakes create waves as large as oceans**, with storms producing 20–30 foot swells.

≋ **Standing water attracts mosquitoes because it lets larvae develop safely**, while moving water disrupts them.

≋ **Fish sense movement through a lateral line**, detecting pressure changes in the water long before danger arrives.

≋ **Rivers create natural fog**, as warmer water meets cold morning air.

≋ **Lake depths can change suddenly**, forming steep underwater cliffs close to shore.

≋ **Some rivers glow faintly at night**, filled with bioluminescent microorganisms.

≋ **Most lakes shrink slowly over thousands of years**, filling with sediment until they become marshes.

≋ **Dams change river temperature**, affecting fish and plant life downstream.

≋ **Waterfalls act like barriers**, preventing species from moving upstream.

≋ **The sound of a river can mask important noises**, making wildlife harder to hear.

≋ **Different fish prefer different types of current**, using slow eddies or fast channels depending on the species.

≋ **You can estimate water clarity using a simple disk**, watching how deep it sinks before disappearing.

≋ **Mud from river bottoms often contains ancient fossils**, washed downstream during floods.

≋ **A lake's "thermocline" acts like a wall**, dividing warm surface water from cold deep water.

≋ **Water pressure increases dramatically with depth**, compressing air spaces in your body.

≋ **Fast-moving rivers often hide deep holes**, carved by swirling water.

MYTHS – BUSTED
RIVERS, LAKES & WATER

MYTHS

Myth #1: "Clear water is safe to drink."
Fact: Pathogens are invisible — **clarity does not equal safety**.

Myth #2: "Rivers always flow south."
Fact: Rivers flow **downhill**, not by compass direction. Some flow north, east, or even in loops.

Myth #3: "Still lakes are lifeless."
Fact: Lakes support **complex ecosystems** from plankton to predators.

Myth #4: "You can't drown in shallow water."
Fact: Strong currents and loss of footing make even shallow areas risky.

Myth #5: "Underwater whirlpools suck people down."
Fact: Most whirlpools are **surface-level** and lose power very quickly underwater.

Myth #6: "Fish can't see humans."
Fact: Many species see **shapes, shadows, and movement** extremely well.

Myth #7: "Frozen lakes are always safe when they look solid."
Fact: Ice varies in thickness depending on currents, springs, and temperature changes.

Myth #8: "River water is coldest at the bottom."
Fact: In summer, deeper water may actually be **warmer** than surface layers.

Myth #9: "If a lake is calm, a storm isn't coming."
Fact: Weather can change water conditions within **minutes**, especially with shifting winds.

Myth #10: "You can swim faster than a river current."
Fact: Strong currents move **faster than even elite swimmers**.

MYTHS & LEGENDS

Many cultures believed rivers were living spirits guiding travelers through the wilderness.

Some legends say lake monsters guard hidden underwater caves.

Old sailors told stories of ghostly lights drifting over marshes, leading wanderers astray.

One myth claims rivers shift their paths to avoid human conflict.

Ancient people believed mountains hid enchanted springs that healed the sick.

Some stories say waterfalls were once doorways to other worlds.

Ch6 – Rivers. Lakes & Water.

MIND-BLOWN™ Cartoons.

LEGENDS
RIVERS, LAKES & WATER
LEGENDS

The Black Dog of the Moors (England)
For centuries, travelers crossing the English moors reported seeing a massive black dog with glowing eyes pacing the edges of footpaths. The creature never barked or attacked — it simply appeared, watched, and faded into the mist. Modern historians point to fog, roaming livestock, and the isolation of the moors, but the legend still unnerves hikers who swear something walks just out of sight.

The Night Marchers of Hawaii
Locals speak of ghostly warrior processions moving along old footpaths on certain nights, drums beating faintly in the distance. Witnesses describe feeling a sudden cold wind or hearing synchronized footsteps before the sounds vanish. Historians believe the stories stem from real ancient trails and ceremonial routes, paired with strong coastal winds that create haunting rhythms. Yet many Hawaiians still avoid known Night Marcher paths after dark.

The Lady in the Light (Chile's Atacama Desert)
Desert travelers told of a glowing woman who appeared at dusk, guiding lost miners toward safety — or deeper into the desert. The Atacama's extreme dryness and temperature swings create mirages that shimmer like human silhouettes, especially around salt flats. But the legend persisted because multiple miners claimed the figure appeared right before life-or-death moments.

The Wendigo Woods of Northern Canada
Loggers and trappers in the far north described a tall, emaciated creature stalking camps during brutal winters. The real fear came

from hearing heavy footsteps in the snow with no tracks visible in the morning. Psychologists now attribute some of these sightings to starvation-induced delirium and extreme cold creating phantom noises. Still, the legend remains one of the most unsettling in the northern forests.

The Screaming Lake of Finland

Villagers near Lake Syväri once swore the water itself screamed on winter nights. The sound was sharp, human-like, and echoed across the ice. Scientists later discovered that expanding and contracting lake ice can create sudden, violent cracks that reverberate like shrieks. Even knowing that, locals admit the sound can still freeze your blood.

The Djinn of the Empty Quarter (Arabian Peninsula)

Nomads crossing the vast desert reported hearing whispers in the dunes and seeing human-shaped shadows standing unnaturally still on dune crests. High winds sweeping across huge sand waves can produce tones that mimic voices, and heat distortions often create tall shifting silhouettes. Still, travelers treat the deep desert with caution, saying the whispers feel too intentional to ignore.

The Shadow Fisher of the Scottish Highlands

Highland anglers told of a dark figure seen at the edges of remote lochs, always standing just beyond clear visibility. The figure never moved but vanished the instant anyone approached. Searchers found nothing but thick fog rolling over the water. Low clouds reflecting moonlight can form tall, still silhouettes — yet centuries of sightings kept the legend alive.

DID YOU KNOW?
RIVERS, LAKES & WATER

Why do rivers look brown after storms?
Because rushing water carries **sediment** and soil downstream.

Why do some lakes whistle in winter?
Expanding ice creates **pressure cracks** that echo across the surface.

Why do rivers have stronger currents on outer bends?
Water moves **faster and deeper** there.

What makes water look blue?
It absorbs **red light**, reflecting shorter blue wavelengths.

Did you know waterfalls create their own wind?
Falling water pushes surrounding air downward, producing a constant breeze at the base.

Did you know cold water can sound higher-pitched than warm water?
Temperature changes alter how sound travels, shifting the tone of splashes and flowing water.

Did you know deep lakes stay cold even in summer?
Sunlight only warms the top layer; deeper water remains trapped in a year-round chill.

Did you know some rivers run backwards during storms?
Strong winds or storm surges can temporarily push water upstream, reversing the flow until pressure balances again.

STORY MOMENT
RIVERS, LAKES & WATER

STORY
MOMENT

I once stopped beside a slow-moving river that looked harmless enough to step into. The surface slid by like lazy glass, barely a ripple in sight, and the warm air made it feel even safer. I kicked off my pack, rolled my shoulders, and decided to wade in a few feet just to cool down. The moment my boot sank past the shallow lip, the current grabbed me harder than I expected — not violently, just firm, steady, and absolutely in control. It was like the river put a hand on my leg and said, *that's far enough.*

I froze, feeling the pull tightening around my ankle. It wasn't going to sweep me under, but it was strong enough to make me reconsider every easy assumption I'd made watching the surface. I backed out slowly, feeling the pressure lessen with each step until I reached the bank again. From there, the river looked exactly the same as before — smooth, quiet, pretending to be gentle.

That's the trick with water. It doesn't need to roar to be dangerous. It waits, patient and silent, letting you believe you're the one in control. And if you're not paying attention, it teaches you — fast — that calm water can still take you off your feet.

QUIZ
RIVERS, LAKES & WATER
QUIZ

Multiple Choice

1. What makes rivers flow?
A. The Moon
B. Gravity
C. Wind
D. Fish movement

2. Why does lake water look blue?
A. Minerals
B. Light absorption
C. Plant color
D. Fish scales

3. What causes lake turnover?
A. Fish migration
B. Boating
C. Seasonal temperature changes
D. Rainfall

4. Why do rivers speed up on outer bends?
A. Rocks
B. Deeper channels
C. Animals
D. Tree roots

5. What makes ice on lakes whistle or boom?
A. Other lakes nearby
B. Thermal expansion

C. Fish movement

D. Air pressure

6. Why is clear water not always safe?

A. It's too cold

B. Pathogens are invisible

C. It moves too fast

D. It lacks minerals

7. What creates a seiche?

A. Boats

B. Wind pushing water to one side

C. Sunlight

D. Fish waves

8. What happens to rivers after storms?

A. They shrink

B. They dry out

C. They carry more sediment

D. They stop moving

9. Why do some rivers "disappear"?

A. Animal digging

B. Underground channels

C. Sunlight

D. Evaporation

10. What is the biggest danger during a flash flood?

A. Fish

B. Temperature

C. Rapid water rise

D. Smell

True or False

1. **Rivers always flow south.**
2. **Lakes can produce dangerous waves.**
3. **Clear water is always safe to drink.**

QUIZ ANSWERS
RIVERS, LAKES & WATER

Multiple Choice

1. **B**

2. **B**

3. **C**

4. **B**

5. **B**

6. **B**

7. **B**

8. **C**

9. **B**

10. **C**

True or False

1. **False**

2. **True**

3. **False**

7

DESERTS & DUNES

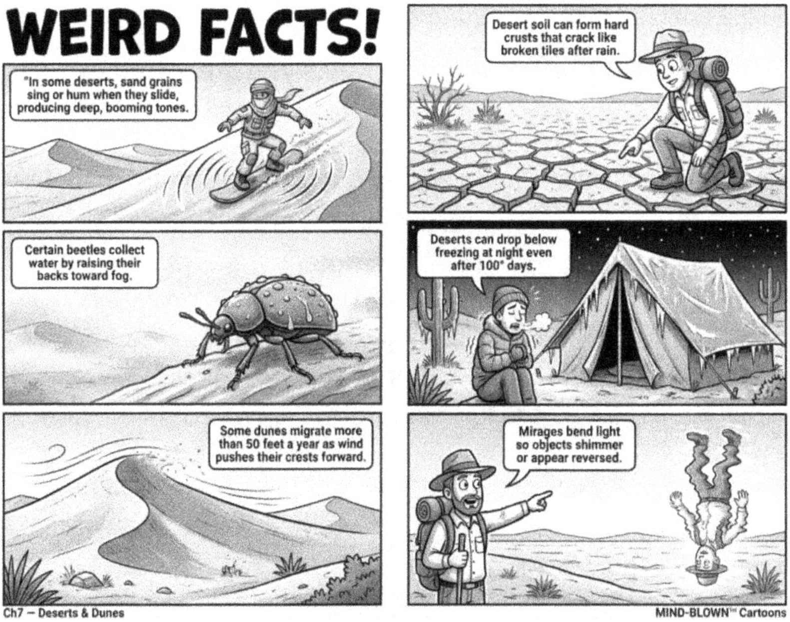

WEIRD & FUN FACTS
Deserts & Dunes

MIND-BLOWN MOMENT

Desert sand can "sing" loud enough to be heard **miles away**, and some dunes boom at over 100 decibels — as loud as a motorcycle — when millions of sand grains slide in perfect unison.

Ancient desert lake beds in the Sahara hide preserved **fossilized whale skeletons**, proof that parts of the desert were once a shallow sea filled with prehistoric marine life.

Some dunes don't just move — they **creep over entire villages**, swallowing buildings so slowly that people hear faint grinding at night as grains shift against stone.

The Atacama Desert has patches of soil so Mars-like that NASA tested **Viking lander instruments** there before sending them to space, because no Earth environment was closer.

Desert thunderstorms can create **dry lightning**, where bolts strike the ground even though rain evaporates before it hits the surface — triggering wildfires with no visible storm.

Certain desert beetles can survive being able to **superheat their bodies** to over 115°F, turning themselves into walking solar collectors without cooking their internal organs.

Some dunes generate electrical charges when sand grains collide, producing tiny **electrostatic sparks** that can shock insects and give a faint crackling sound during windstorms.

☀️ The Sahara Desert sometimes receives **snowfall**, and satellite photos have captured its dunes streaked with white — caused by rare cold snaps pushing down from the Atlas Mountains.

☀️ The Gobi Desert holds "mogotes," hidden pockets of **permafrost** that stay frozen underground even during sweltering summers, creating bizarre icy oases beneath the heat.

☀️ Desert fog in places like the Namib can carry enough moisture to support entire ecosystems, and some plants literally **drink the fog** by funneling condensed droplets into their roots.

☀️ Ancient petrified forests lie buried under dunes, where trees from long-lost ecosystems turned to stone and now appear as polished trunks and logs exposed by shifting sands.

☀️ Sandstorms can charge the air so intensely that they create **glowing halos** around objects, a phenomenon early travelers called "ghost fire" or "desert lightning."

☀️ A single strong windstorm can move more sand in a day than a river moves sediment in a year, reshaping dunes so dramatically that explorers once believed they "rearranged themselves overnight."

☀️ The Sahara experiences massive **dust tsunamis**, walls of airborne sand that can rise thousands of feet into the atmosphere and block out the sun for hours.

☀️ Some lizards in the Arabian Peninsula use "thermal dancing," lifting each foot in sequence so rapidly that it looks like they're tap-dancing to avoid burning themselves on scorching sand.

☀️ Desert night skies are so clear that distant galaxies are visible without telescopes, making some deserts the **darkest places on Earth** outside of the ocean.

Hidden beneath some dunes are ancient burial grounds and abandoned cities, preserved by dry air so completely that artifacts remain **untouched for thousands of years**.

Certain desert ants navigate using internal "sky compasses," memorizing the position of the sun to return home in perfectly straight lines even after chaotic scavenging runs.

The world's largest desert isn't the Sahara — it's **Antarctica**, an ice desert that receives less precipitation than the driest hot deserts on Earth.

Some desert rocks move on their own, leaving long trails behind them. These **sailing stones** glide when thin sheets of ice and wind combine perfectly, making them look alive.

Rapid desert flash floods can carve **new canyons in a single afternoon**, slicing through rock with the power of a natural demolition team.

Certain desert spiders create "rolling webs" — circular traps they release during sandstorms that tumble like wheels to capture smaller insects blown across the dunes.

Wind erosion reveals enormous underground cave networks, forming skylights in the desert floor where collapsed ceilings expose caverns that once held ancient rivers.

Some desert sands contain magnetic minerals that align in patterns, creating **natural desert compasses** early travelers unknowingly used to stay oriented.

Satellite scans show parts of the Sahara still hold massive **underground aquifers**, ancient lakes the size of small seas trapped far below the surface.

☀ Snake trails on dunes leave perfect **sine-wave signatures**, and trackers can tell the hour and temperature of movement just by reading the sharpness of the curves.

☀ The driest regions on Earth still receive moisture from **space dust**, tiny particles that settle from the upper atmosphere and influence how clouds form in desert air.

☀ Some deserts produce **shadowless days**, where the Sun sits so high overhead that objects cast almost no visible shadow at all.

☀ Sand in extreme deserts can fuse into **natural glass** during intense lightning strikes, creating twisting, rootlike structures called fulgurites that can stretch several feet long beneath the surface.

☀ The Sahara still hides giant **fossilized river channels** visible only from space — evidence of massive waterways that once rivaled the Mississippi.

☀ Certain desert plants release chemicals that **poison surrounding soil** so nothing grows nearby, giving themselves a survival buffer known as allelopathy.

☀ Some desert regions pulse with strange, rhythmic ground vibrations caused by **distant earthquake waves** traveling thousands of miles through the Earth's crust.

☀ The Atacama is so dry that uncovered metal objects left out for decades barely rust, making it one of the few places where **decay almost pauses**.

☀ In the Namib Desert, beetles and spiders follow **thermal shadows** cast by dunes to avoid overheating, moving in sync with the slope's shifting shade.

Tiny crustaceans called fairy shrimp lie dormant in desert salt flats for years, reviving only when sudden rain turns the ground into **temporary oceans**.

Massive star dunes — the tallest dunes on Earth — grow in deserts where wind comes from multiple directions, creating **pyramids of sand** thousands of feet high.

Some desert rocks emit faint **moonlight glows** at night thanks to reflected starlight and their unique mineral surfaces, a phenomenon called albedo shine.

The world's hottest reliably recorded ground temperature, 201°F, occurred in the desert at Furnace Creek — hot enough to **fry an egg on sand** in seconds.

Ancient desert travelers could tell time by listening to distant dunes: when sand cooled just right, the shifting layers caused subtle **grain avalanches** that signaled dusk.

Many desert animals use **infrared vision** to detect heat trails left behind by prey on scorching surfaces — effectively tracking "thermal footprints."

The Sahara breathes: its borders expand and contract dramatically every few decades due to **monsoon cycle shifts**, sometimes growing or shrinking by hundreds of miles.

NASA found microorganisms in the Atacama that can survive solely on **trace atmospheric moisture**, making them candidates for surviving Mars-like conditions.

Some deserts create **false dawns**, a brightening of the horizon caused by sunlight reflecting off interplanetary dust — a rare phenomenon called zodiacal light.

Dune slipfaces can collapse with enough force to create miniature **sand avalanches** that travel faster than a person can sprint downhill.

Ancient petroglyphs in the Arabian deserts show giraffes, hippos, and swimming humans — carved during a time when much of the desert was **lush savanna**.

Salt in desert flats can crystallize into geometric patterns, forming **natural mosaics** that shift after each rare rainfall.

Certain scorpions can lower their metabolism so drastically they survive on **one insect per year**, waiting motionless under sand for months at a time.

Saharan dust storms release so much airborne iron and phosphorus that it fertilizes the **Amazon Rainforest**, feeding ecosystems an ocean away.

Desert temperatures can spike 50 degrees in minutes during sudden chinook winds, creating **instant heat waves** that stun wildlife.

Some dunes produce **double shadows** at sunrise due to light refracting through airborne dust layers, making objects appear to have ghostlike outlines.

MYTHS – BUSTED
Deserts & Dunes

Myth #1: "Deserts are always scorching hot."
Fact: Many deserts freeze at night or during winter because **dry air loses heat quickly**.

Myth #2: "Mirages are pools of water."
Fact: Mirages are **light refractions**, bending images of the sky down toward your eyes.

Myth #3: "Nothing lives in deserts."
Fact: Deserts are filled with **specialized plants and animals** that thrive under extreme conditions.

Myth #4: "Cacti store water you can drink."
Fact: Most cactus fluid is **toxic or acidic**, causing dehydration instead of solving it.

Myth #5: "Sand dunes stay in place."
Fact: Dunes can move **several feet per year**, shifting with seasons and storms.

Myth #6: "You can navigate by sun alone in a desert."
Fact: Heat distortion and lack of visual markers make navigation extremely unreliable.

Myth #7: "Digging straight down always finds water."
Fact: Water in deserts is rare and often **deep, salty, or contaminated**.

Myth #8: "Scorpions attack unprovoked."
Fact: Most scorpions avoid conflict and sting only when **stepped on or cornered**.

Myth #9: "Sandstorms completely bury people."
Fact: Sandstorms mainly move fine dust; the danger is **choking, disorientation, and debris**, not burial.

Myth #10: "Desert snakes chase people."
Fact: Snakes conserve energy — they avoid humans and escape whenever possible.

Ch7 — Deserts & Dunes · MIND-BLOWN™ Cartoons

LEGENDS
Deserts & Dunes

LEGENDS

The Lost Caravan of the Empty Quarter

Nomads tell of a massive caravan that vanished without a trace in the Rub' al Khali, seen last heading toward a low dune ridge before a sandstorm swallowed it whole. Travelers claim that on windless nights you can hear the faint clinking of camel bells drifting through the dunes. Shifting sands and sudden dune collapses likely buried the entire party, sealing it beneath layers of sand deeper than a building.

The Whispering Wells of the Sahara

Old guides speak of certain desert wells that "whisper" at night, sending soft voices spiraling upward from the darkness. Anyone leaning in hears distant murmurs like buried conversations. The truth lies in underground chambers where temperature shifts push air through narrow fissures, creating haunting, voice-like vibrations that echo up the stone shafts.

The Phantom Rider of Wadi Rum

Bedouin travelers report seeing a lone rider crossing distant dunes at twilight — a tall figure on a pale camel that leaves no tracks. The rider glides along with impossible speed before fading into rising heat haze. The phenomenon lines up with distant mirages and refracted silhouettes, magnifying travelers beyond the horizon until they appear ghostlike and weightless.

The Singing Caves of the Namib
Explorers described caves in remote dune fields that hum like distant choirs when storms approach. The sound can build to a deep, vibrating drone that rolls across the desert floor. These "songs" come from wind pressure pushing through tight volcanic tubes, but the effect is eerie enough that locals still avoid these caves after sunset.

The Sand Walker of the White Desert
Travelers in Egypt's White Desert speak of a tall, chalk-white figure that appears only in moonlight, motionless on a distant ridge. Approach it, and it seems to shift sideways like a glitch in the landscape. The desert's towering chalk formations create perfect human-shaped silhouettes, and swirling moon shadows make them appear to move even when the ground is perfectly still.

The Vanished Village of Ubar
Arabian lore tells of a trading city swallowed overnight by the desert after its people ignored warnings from wandering travelers. When explorers finally located Ubar's ruins, they found collapsed ground where limestone caverns caved in, pulling buildings into a sinkhole system. The story of a city "punished by the desert" started with a real geological disaster powerful enough to erase an entire settlement.

The Burning Road of the Lut Desert
Locals once claimed a "black road of fire" appeared across the plains during extreme heat, stretching to the horizon like a glowing path. The effect came from superheated air bending light along dark volcanic rock beds, turning them into shimmering, molten-looking ribbons that pulse as if alive.

The Night Drummer of the Atacama
Campers in the Atacama have long reported rhythmic drumming sounds echoing across salt flats after midnight — slow, steady pulses that seem too patterned to be natural. Scientists later found that as salt crusts cool, they expand and crack in rhythmic sequences, producing eerie, drumlike pops that roll across the empty landscape.

The Stone Guardian of the Gobi
Nomads describe a massive stone figure that appears on high ridges, watching travelers from a distance. It never moves, yet it never seems to be in the same place twice. The shifting position comes from massive, human-shaped basalt pillars created by ancient volcanic eruptions. As dunes migrate, these pillars appear, disappear, and reappear miles away, unsettling anyone unfamiliar with the terrain.

The Dune Lights of the Mojave
Rangers and travelers have reported floating orbs of light drifting low across the Mojave at night — silent, pale, and unpredictable. Many follow the same path for minutes before vanishing. The phenomenon is tied to rare pockets of bioluminescent insects combined with temperature inversion layers that amplify and distort tiny points of light into ghostlike floating spheres.

DID YOU KNOW?
Deserts & Dunes

Did you know some desert valleys generate their own **gravity-driven winds**, where cold air suddenly pours downslope like a slow invisible avalanche, blasting sand for hours even when the sky is clear?

Did you know certain deserts preserve **ancient footprints for thousands of years**, with trails from humans, mammoths, and giant sloths still visible because there's no rain to erase them?

Did you know dunes can create **standing waves** in the atmosphere — invisible walls of stable air — that migrating birds use like ramps to glide across entire desert regions with almost no effort?

Did you know that some deserts contain **microbial mats** living several inches below the sand, surviving with almost no water by extracting moisture directly from humid night air?

Did you know the Sahara produces dust storms so massive they inject nutrients into the **Atlantic hurricane system**, quietly influencing the severity and frequency of storms an ocean away?

Did you know desert varnish — the dark coating on rocks — forms so slowly that a layer the thickness of a human hair may take hundreds of years, turning boulders into **natural climate history records**?

Did you know some deserts have **underground labyrinths** of ancient lava tubes large enough to hide entire ecosystems, with stable temperatures and faint moisture supporting insects and rare microbes?

Did you know giant star dunes can act like **acoustic amplifiers**, taking a whisper at their base and projecting it up the slope so it sounds like a voice answering from above?

Did you know that during rare desert rains, certain seeds germinate, bloom, and die within **24 hours**, completing an entire life cycle before the ground dries again?

Did you know sand can become so superheated during extreme events that it forms **synthetic minerals** normally created only by asteroid impacts — making parts of desert surfaces chemically similar to lunar soil?

Did you know entire desert regions can experience **"phantom rain,"** where storm clouds dump moisture that evaporates mid-air before hitting the ground, creating the illusion of rain columns dissolving into nothing?

Did you know some desert mountains trigger **thermal updraft pillars** so strong that they can lift insects, seeds, and even lightweight debris thousands of feet into the sky, forming drifting "sky rivers" of life?

Did you know infrared satellites have revealed **hidden fossil river networks** beneath several major deserts, showing that massive waterways once crossed areas now considered among the driest on Earth?

STORY MOMENT
Deserts & Dunes

STORY MOMENT

I once hiked into a stretch of desert that looked completely ordinary — just a long spine of dunes and heat rippling off the ground. The kind of place you think you understand after five minutes. By late afternoon the sun was dropping behind a ridge, and the whole place glowed like someone had turned the world to bronze. I climbed a tall dune to get my bearings, and when I reached the top, the wind shifted — not a gust, not a breeze... just a sudden change in direction that felt almost intentional.

Below me, the sand started to move.
Not blow — **move**.

At first it looked like shadows sliding across the slope, but then the sound hit: a deep, rolling vibration coming from inside the dune, like the earth was clearing its throat. The entire face of sand began to tremble, and a long sheet of grains broke loose, collapsing in one massive slide. And with it came a sound I will never forget — a low, booming note that echoed across the valley like someone striking a buried drum the size of a house.

People talk about "singing dunes."
This wasn't singing.
This was **the desert speaking**.

The dune kept humming as the sand settled, waves of vibration pulsing under my boots. Then it faded — suddenly, completely — leaving that vast, impossible silence in its place. I walked down the slope feeling smaller, sharper, and very aware that the desert doesn't need storms or danger to overwhelm you. Sometimes all it takes is a moment you can't explain.

QUIZ
Deserts & Dunes

QUIZ

Multiple Choice

1. What causes mirages in deserts?
A. Reflections from sand
B. Light bending between hot and cool air
C. Underground heat
D. Moonlight

2. Why do desert temperatures drop so quickly at night?
A. Cold sand
B. Dry air loses heat fast
C. Winds increase
D. Animals absorb heat

3. What makes dunes migrate?
A. Earthquakes
B. Rivers
C. Wind
D. Animals

4. Why are many desert animals nocturnal?
A. Food is sweeter at night
B. Night is safer and cooler
C. Sunlight blinds them
D. They avoid predators only

5. What creates "singing dunes"?
A. Birds
B. Sand grains vibrating

C. Heat cracking rocks

D. Distant traffic

6. Why can sandstorms be dangerous?

A. Sudden cold

B. Flying debris and disorientation

C. Wild animals

D. Rain

7. What defines a desert?

A. Heat

B. Sand

C. Low rainfall

D. No plants

8. Why can cactus water be harmful?

A. It's salty

B. It contains toxins

C. It's frozen

D. It evaporates too fast

9. What causes desert "blooms"?

A. Temperature

B. Moon cycles

C. Rare rainfall

D. Wind direction

10. Why do sandfish lizards "swim" under sand?

A. It's cooler

B. They can't walk

C. It helps them hunt

D. They avoid sunlight

Fill-in-the-Blank

1. A desert is defined by low _____.

2. A dune moves when wind pushes sand up the _____ side.

3. Mirages happen when light bends between layers of hot and _____ air.

4. Cactus fluid is often unsafe because it contains _____.

5. Desert nights get cold because air holds almost no _____.

WEIRD FACTS!

Some deserts are made entirely of salt, not sand—remains of ancient dried seas.

Desert varnish on rocks forms slower than paint drying—microns per century.

Desert plants like creosote can clone themselves into rings thousands of years old.

Camel humps store fat, not water—they burn it for energy.

Dust storms can rise thousands of feet and travel across oceans.

Desert thunderstorms can drop rain that evaporates before hitting the ground.

Ch7 — Deserts & Dunes

MIND-BLOWN™ Cartoons

QUIZ ANSWERS
Deserts & Dunes

Multiple Choice

1. **B**

2. **B**

3. **C**

4. **B**

5. **B**

6. **B**

7. **C**

8. **B**

9. **C**

10. **A**

Fill-in-the-Blank

1. **Rainfall**

2. **Windward**

3. **Cool**

4. **Toxins**

5. **Heat**

000

8

NATIONAL PARKS

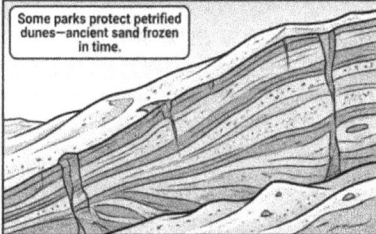

WEIRD & FUN FACTS
NATIONAL PARKS

MIND-BLOWN MOMENT

- **Yellowstone has more geysers than the rest of the world combined**, thanks to its massive underground hotspot.

- **The Grand Canyon is so deep that it creates its own weather**, with temperature swings between rim and river often reaching 30 degrees.

- **The Great Smoky Mountains get their signature haze from plant vapors**, not pollution.

- **Yosemite's granite cliffs were once deep underground**, formed from cooled magma later exposed by erosion.

- **The tallest trees on Earth grow in Redwood National and State Parks**, rising over 350 feet.

- **The world's oldest trees live in Great Basin National Park**, where bristlecone pines can exceed 4,000 years.

- **Joshua Tree National Park is actually where two deserts meet**, the Mojave and Colorado.

- **Hot Springs National Park was first protected for its water**, not its scenery.

- **Crater Lake formed when a volcano collapsed**, leaving behind a deep basin filled only with rain and snow.

- **Glacier National Park once had over 100 glaciers**, but climate shifts have reduced their number dramatically.

- **Denali is the tallest mountain in North America**, towering above the Alaskan landscape.

🏔 **The deepest cave in the U.S. is in South Dakota**, inside Jewel Cave National Monument.

🏔 **Bryce Canyon is not a canyon**, but a collection of natural amphitheaters filled with hoodoos.

🏔 **Zion's Emerald Pools form from water filtering slowly through sandstone**, taking months or even years to emerge.

🏔 **Death Valley holds the hottest temperature ever recorded**, reaching 134°F in 1913.

🏔 **Big Bend National Park protects some of the darkest skies in America**, free from light pollution.

🏔 **Sequoia trees can survive fire**, using their thick bark and heat-activated cones to thrive.

🏔 **The Everglades is a slow-moving river**, not a swamp.

🏔 **Acadia National Park's Cadillac Mountain sees the first sunrise in the U.S.** for part of the year.

🏔 **The Tetons rise sharply because they were uplifted without forming foothills**, creating dramatic peaks.

🏔 **The Great Lakes can create waves as big as small oceans**, especially during storms.

🏔 **Lake Clark National Park in Alaska protects active volcanoes**, huge lakes, and enormous brown bears.

🏔 **Hawaii Volcanoes National Park contains lava flows that create new land**, extending the island coastline.

🏔 **Kings Canyon in California rivals the Grand Canyon in depth**, though it's carved from a different type of rock.

🏔 **Petrified Forest National Park contains trees turned to stone**, preserved for over 200 million years.

🏔 **Mammoth Cave National Park contains the longest cave system on Earth**, with over 400 miles mapped.

🔺 **Mount Rainier's glaciers feed five major rivers**, shaping the entire region.

🔺 **Badlands National Park is filled with fossils**, including ancient horses, rhinos, and saber-toothed predators.

🔺 **Arches National Park loses arches naturally**, as erosion eventually weakens their supports.

🔺 **Channel Islands National Park contains species found nowhere else**, thanks to long-term isolation.

🔺 **Banff National Park's lakes glow turquoise**, reflecting glacial rock particles suspended in the water.

🔺 **Serengeti National Park hosts the world's largest mammal migration**, with wildebeest covering hundreds of miles.

🔺 **Torres del Paine in Chile has jagged granite towers**, shaped by millions of years of glacial carving.

🔺 **Plitvice Lakes National Park forms waterfalls continuously**, as mineral-rich water builds new natural dams.

🔺 **Kruger National Park in South Africa is larger than some countries**, protecting iconic African wildlife.

🔺 **Uluru in Australia changes color throughout the day**, glowing red, orange, and purple depending on sunlight.

🔺 **Fiordland National Park in New Zealand holds long glacial fjords**, carved deep into mountain valleys.

🔺 **Vatnajökull National Park in Iceland covers volcanoes, glaciers, and black-sand plains**, all within one region.

🔺 **Norway's Jotunheimen National Park is home to giants in Viking mythology**, with peaks once believed to be sleeping stone beings.

🔺 **Some European parks protect both nature and villages**, blending culture and wilderness.

🔺 **Chile's Conguillío National Park has forests growing on fresh lava flows**, where life returns surprisingly fast.

🔺 **Japan's national parks include volcanic islands**, hot springs, snowy ranges, and dense cedar forests.

🔺 **Many African and South American parks use controlled burning**, keeping grasslands healthy.

🔺 **Lake Superior's national lakeshores preserve over 300 shipwrecks** from the Great Lakes shipping era.

🔺 **Spain's Picos de Europa National Park contains some of the deepest vertical caves**, dropping thousands of feet.

🔺 **Yosemite's firefall phenomenon happens now only naturally**, when setting sun lights up Horsetail Fall in February.

🔺 **Yellowstone's geysers** are so interconnected underground that when one major geyser erupts, pressure waves ripple through the system and can **change the eruption schedule** of geysers miles away.

🔺 **Great Sand Dunes National Park** sits atop a massive hidden aquifer, and when you stomp on some wet sand patches, the ground **vibrates like a drum**, a rare phenomenon called "booming sand."

🔺 **Katmai's Valley of Ten Thousand Smokes** was created by the largest volcanic eruption of the 20th century, producing ash flows so hot they **sterilized entire river systems** for years.

🔺 Some quartz-sandstone pillars in **China's Zhangjiajie National Forest Park** are so tall and narrow they create their own swirling **thermal vortices**, pulling mist upward in spirals that look like smoke signals.

🔺 In **Namibia's Namib-Naukluft National Park**, beetles survive by harvesting water straight from fog, using microscopic bumps on their shells that **pull moisture from the air** like living condensation traps.

MYTHS – BUSTED
NATIONAL PARKS

MYTHS

Myth #1: "National parks are untouched wilderness."
Fact: Parks balance **preservation and human impact**, with managed trails, controlled burns, and wildlife monitoring.

Myth #2: "Bears hibernate all winter without waking."
Fact: Bears enter **torpor**, waking up periodically and even moving dens.

Myth #3: "Wild animals near people are friendly."
Fact: Animals in parks remain **fully wild**, even if they appear calm.

Myth #4: "If a trail is marked, you can't get lost."
Fact: Fog, snow, side paths, and fatigue cause hikers to stray every year.

Myth #5: "Feeding wildlife helps them."
Fact: Fed animals become sick, dependent, or aggressive.

Myth #6: "Rangers mostly give directions."
Fact: Rangers handle rescues, research, fires, law enforcement, and wildlife protection.

Myth #7: "Big parks matter more than small ones."
Fact: Small parks often protect **rare ecosystems or species** found nowhere else.

Myth #8: "Lakes in parks are clean enough to drink from."
Fact: Many contain **giardia, bacteria, and parasites**.

Myth #9: "You can explore anywhere inside a park."
Fact: Sensitive areas are closed to protect **habitats, artifacts, and endangered species**.

Myth #10: "All national parks are crowded."
Fact: Many remain rugged and remote, with vast areas rarely visited.

Myth #11: "Campfires are allowed everywhere."
Fact: Many parks restrict fires due to **drought, wildlife, or forest health**.

Myth #12: "Mountains inside parks don't change."
Fact: They erode constantly and reshape valleys through **slides and freeze-thaw cycles**.

Myth #13: "Forests in parks are natural."
Fact: Many grew after logging before park creation.

Myth #14: "Rivers in parks stay the same each year."
Fact: Rivers shift channels, deposit new sediment, and carve new bends.

Myth #15: "Animals won't approach campsites."
Fact: They will — especially if drawn by **smell or food scraps**.

Myth #16: "National park boundaries never change."
Fact: They often expand, shrink, or become connected through conservation projects.

Myth #17: "Storms don't hit desert parks."
Fact: Deserts get **violent flash floods**.

Myth #18: "Visitors cause most problems."
Fact: Weather, erosion, and natural events often reshape parks more than people do.

Myth #19: "Glaciers in parks are permanent."
Fact: Many are shrinking rapidly each decade.

Myth #20: "Trees in protected parks never burn."
Fact: Fire is a **required** process for many forests.

Myth #21: "Geysers erupt on a fixed schedule."
Fact: Many geysers change frequency depending on **underground water levels**.

Myth #22: "All caves are safe if they're in parks."
Fact: Caves can contain **bad air, tight passages, and sudden drops**.

Myth #23: "International parks work like U.S. parks."
Fact: Some protect culture, villages, and farming alongside nature.

Myth #24: "The biggest wildlife is always the most dangerous."
Fact: Small animals (like deer and raccoons) cause more accidents than predators.

WEIRD FACTS!

Some parks preserve entire fossilized forests still standing upright.

Some cave formations grow one tiny drop at a time.

Some geysers blast water higher than a ten-story building.

Some park lakes are so clear, you can see over 100 feet down.

Ch 8 — National Parks

MIND-BLOWN™ Cartoons

LEGENDS
NATIONAL PARKS

LEGENDS

Deep Lake That "Breathes" at Night — Glacier National Park

Some backcountry rangers insist a hidden alpine lake rises and falls after dark, as if something beneath the surface is slowly inhaling and exhaling. The waterline lifts in smooth pulses, then sinks again without wind, waves, or wildlife. Scientists blame trapped subglacial springs that release pressure in cycles, but many swear the movement feels too steady — too alive — for simple hydraulics.

The Whistling Caves — Grand Canyon National Park

Hikers exploring remote side canyons describe a high, melodic whistling drifting from deep within narrow cave cracks. The sound bends and changes pitch as if a voice is trying to form words. Park geologists attribute it to rapid pressure changes inside the rock chambers, but desert guides claim it's the echo of ancient spirits still "walking the stone corridors."

The Spirit Moose — Isle Royale National Park

For generations, visitors have reported a massive snow-white moose appearing in the island's dense fog. It moves silently between trees, towering above normal bulls, and vanishes without sound or tracks. No photograph has ever captured it clearly, leading some to believe it's not an animal at all — but a forest guardian that chooses when, and to whom, it appears.

131

The Vanishing Campsite — Yosemite National Park

A recurring legend speaks of a perfectly arranged but abandoned campsite deep in the backcountry: tent pitched, cookware set, fire ring built — all intact, all untouched. Rangers who search for it can never locate the same spot twice. Many believe shifting granite acoustics and valley mirages create the illusion, but others think the campsite itself "moves" with the forest.

The Ridge Watchers — Big Bend National Park

Night hikers report tall, unmoving silhouettes standing on distant ridgelines — silent figures that never shift or sway. They remain fixed for hours, then disappear the moment someone looks away or blinks. Locals say the desert holds "old watchers" who track anyone crossing the basin after dark, though scientists chalk it up to distant hoodoos casting deceptive moonlit shadows.

The Trembling Ground — Yellowstone National Park

Certain geothermal basins emit deep rhythmic pulses you feel through your boots, as if the very crust is breathing beneath you. Rangers say the tremors come from subsurface magma shifting through fractures, but the pulses sometimes sync perfectly with human footsteps — a sensation many describe as "being noticed" from below.

The Phantom Campfire — Great Smoky Mountains National Park

Travelers occasionally smell woodsmoke or hear a faint crackling fire on trails where campfires are forbidden. When they search, they find only circles of cold ash that crumble like dust at the slightest touch. Weather patterns explain the drifting scent, but no one has accounted for the ash rings that appear and vanish as if someone camped there moments before.

The Wind That Calls Your Name — Denali National Park
Climbers on high ridges sometimes hear sudden gusts that sound startlingly like human voices calling their names. The phenomenon happens even on still, starry nights with no storm activity. Scientists blame katabatic airflow blending with rock acoustics, but Alaskan guides warn newcomers not to answer — "the mountain tests you," they say.

The Staircase to Nowhere — Olympic National Park
Hidden deep in the rainforest, explorers tell of a moss-coated stone staircase rising up a small hill — perfectly preserved yet leading into empty air. No structure exists around it, and the stones remain icy cold even in warm weather. Some believe it's a remnant of an abandoned homestead; others whisper it's the last trace of something far older than the park itself.

The Canyon That Steals Echoes — Zion National Park
A particular bend in the canyon is said to swallow sound entirely — shouts, claps, and even whistles vanish without echo. Hikers claim that minutes later, they hear faint versions of their own words whispered back from the canyon walls behind them. Geologists cite unique acoustic absorption, but visitors regularly report a "presence" listening from the stone.

The Lantern Walker — Shenandoah National Park
Ridge hikers have spotted a lone lantern light gliding along the trail on moonless nights. Unlike a human step, the light never bobs or sways — it moves smoothly, like floating. Rangers who attempt to follow the glow always find the trail empty and silent, with no footprints and no sign of any traveler.

The Footsteps in the Sand — Joshua Tree National Park
Solo hikers sometimes hear a measured crunching of footsteps behind them on windless desert nights. When they stop, the unseen steps stop. Turning around reveals only perfect, untouched sand stretching to the horizon. Experts point to thermal contractions making rocks crack, but locals insist the desert keeps its own kind of company.

The Echo That Arrives Before You Speak — Arches National Park
Explorers in remote arches tell of an impossible phenomenon: a faint echo arriving *before* a sound is made. Hikers have reported hearing the ghost of their own voice whispering from a distant wall a split second before they actually speak. Acoustic experts claim certain arch shapes can bounce environmental noise in unpredictable ways — but that doesn't explain hikers hearing their *own* voice early, nor the fact that the "pre-echo" never matches the exact tone of the real one.

MIND-BLOWN™ Cartoons

DID YOU KNOW?
NATIONAL PARKS

Which U.S. park is the most visited?
Great Smoky Mountains National Park.

What park is home to the world's largest cave system?
Mammoth Cave National Park.

Which park has the highest peak in North America?
Denali National Park.

Which park contains Half Dome and El Capitan?
Yosemite.

What causes Yellowstone's colors?
Heat-loving **microbes** called thermophiles.

Which park has the tallest dunes in North America?
Great Sand Dunes National Park.

Where can you see volcanic land forming in real time?
Hawaii Volcanoes National Park.

Which park protects ancient bristlecone pine trees?
Great Basin.

Which African park hosts the Great Migration?
Serengeti.

Which park features bright turquoise lakes caused by rock flour?
Banff.

Which U.S. park protects giant saguaro cacti?
Saguaro National Park.

What is the deepest lake in the U.S.?
Crater Lake.

Which park is known for its hoodoos?
Bryce Canyon.

Which park contains world-famous slot canyons?
Zion.

What park protects mangrove forests and crocodiles?
Everglades.

Which park contains the Painted Desert?
Petrified Forest.

Which park's valleys were carved by glaciers?
Glacier and Yosemite.

Which park lies inside a volcanic caldera?
Crater Lake.

Which European park features steep fjords?
Norway's Jostedalsbreen.

Which Croatian park has stair-step waterfalls?
Plitvice Lakes.

Which park is known for black bears casually crossing roads?
Great Smoky Mountains.

Which national park is located on five separate islands?
Channel Islands National Park.

STORY MOMENT
NATIONAL PARKS

The Sky That Wouldn't Stay Still

The night started normal enough. Cool air. Dry pine needles. A sky so clear it looked freshly polished. I was camping along a high ridge locals called *The Balcony* because the view stretched forever. But around midnight, something shifted—subtle, easy to miss.

The sky... moved. Not the stars—**the darkness between them.** A faint ripple, like heat distortion, sliding across the night in air too cold for mirages. I froze. No wind. No distant planes. The whole forest held its breath. Even the insects stopped.

It happened again: a smooth wave crossing from west to east, bending the blackness. My phone couldn't focus—like it didn't know how far away the universe was. As it passed overhead, I felt a brief pressure in my chest, and every metal piece on my pack gave a tiny *ping*, as if something brushed through them.

A third ripple rolled overhead, and this time the stars behind it lagged—light chasing the distortion like it was outrunning starlight itself. That shouldn't happen anywhere except a physics experiment. Definitely not in a silent forest at midnight.

Then, suddenly, it ended. A blast of cold wind pushed through, the trees exhaled, and the insects snapped back online like someone flipped a switch.

Morning looked normal. My phone showed nothing. No proof at all—except the metal zipper pull on my pack. Overnight it had twisted, not bent but **spiraled**, like something gripped it and spun it half a turn. I tried recreating it with pliers. No chance.

137

I go back to that ridge sometimes, waiting to see it again. Maybe it was a rare atmospheric wave. Maybe something magnetic. Or maybe the sky isn't as empty—or as stable—as we like to believe.

And here's the strange part: ever since that night, when the sky shimmers before a storm, I feel that same pressure in my chest. Like something up there remembers... and hasn't finished whatever it started.

WEIRD FACTS!

"Some park trees have been alive for over 2,000 years."

"Certain parks sit on magnetic anomalies that confuse compasses."

"Rock arches can form over millions of years—then collapse suddenly."

"Rock arches can form over millions of years—then collapse suddenly."

"Some mud pots are heated by magma close to the surface."

"Some park trees have been alive for over 2,000 years."

"Rock arches can form over of years—then collapse suddenly."

"Some mud pots are heated by magma close to the surface."

Ch 8 — National Parks

MIND-BLOWN™ Cartoons

QUIZ
NATIONAL PARKS

QUIZ

Multiple Choice

1. What makes Yellowstone's geothermal features possible?
A. Wind
B. A volcanic hotspot
C. Groundwater springs
D. Soil erosion

2. Why are Banff's lakes turquoise?
A. Algae
B. Rock flour
C. Reflection
D. Minerals

3. What causes the hoodoos in Bryce Canyon?
A. Volcanic eruptions
B. Freeze-thaw cycles
C. Animal digging
D. Wind only

4. What causes the Smoky Mountains' misty appearance?
A. Pollution
B. Plant vapors
C. Rising dust
D. Fog machines

5. What causes singing dunes?

A. Animals

B. Vibrating sand grains

C. Echoes

D. Wind tunnels

6. Why is the Grand Canyon colorful?

A. Painted minerals

B. Rocks from different eras

C. Moss

D. Air pollution

7. Why do rangers close certain areas?

A. To annoy visitors

B. To protect sensitive habitats

C. To hide wildlife

D. For decoration

8. What produces Crater Lake?

A. Melting glaciers

B. A collapsed volcano

C. Rain runoff

D. A drained river

9. Why do some parks use controlled burns?

A. To clear campsites

B. To maintain ecosystem health

C. To warm animals

D. For tourist interest

10. What creates slot canyons like those in Zion?

A. Flash floods

B. Earthquakes

C. Lava

D. Tree roots

BRYCE CANYON
NATIONAL PARK

MIND-BLOWN™
Images

QUIZ ANSWERS
NATIONAL PARKS

Multiple Choice

1. **B**

2. **B**

3. **B**

4. **B**

5. **B**

6. **B**

7. **B**

8. **B**

9. **B**

10. **A**

MIND-BLOWN

9

DANGEROUS
OUTDOORS

WEIRD FACTS!

"Some lakes can explode without warning — releasing enough trapped CO_2 to suffocate everything within miles."

"Mountain canyons can create wind tunnels where gusts exceed 100 mph — even on calm days."

"Before a lightning strike, your entire body can become electrically charged — a silent warning seconds before impact."

"Lightning can strike the ground miles away from the bolt — the ground current kills more people than lightning itself."

CH 9 — DANGEROUS OUTDOORS

MIND-BLOWN™ Cartoons

WEIRD & FUN FACTS DANGEROUS OUTDOORS

⚠ Some deserts drop below freezing in a single hour.
Hot air disappears fast after sunset because dry air can't hold heat.

⚠ Flash floods can travel faster than you can sprint.
Steep terrain funnels water into narrow channels, building speed instantly.

⚠ Rivers can look calm on top while ripping underneath.
Hidden currents move faster along the bottom, creating deadly "foot traps."

⚠ Moose injure more people each year than bears.
They're huge, surprisingly fast, and extremely territorial.

⚠ Heatstroke can happen even when it's only 75°F.
High humidity blocks your sweat from evaporating.

⚠ Cold water steals body heat 25 times faster than cold air.
Water pulls heat directly from your skin.

⚠ Wind can pick up 50 mph in minutes during mountain storms.
Warm valley air rises and crashes into cold mountain air.

⚠ Some snakes can still bite after they're dead.
Their nervous system fires reflexively for hours.

⚠ Lightning can strike from 10 miles away, even under clear sky.
"Bolt from the blue" happens when charge travels sideways before dropping.

⚠ Avalanches can reach highway speeds.
Snow layers collapse, trapping air that makes the slide accelerate.

144

⚠ **Sand dunes can "boom" like drums.**
Vibrating grains rub together in dry conditions.

⚠ **Quicksand isn't deadly unless you panic.**
It's dense enough to hold you, but you float if you lean back.

⚠ **Trees can explode in wildfires.**
Sap inside superheats and bursts like a pressure cooker.

⚠ **Snow blindness is literally a sunburn on your eyeballs.**
Bright snow reflects UV light into unprotected eyes.

⚠ **Mountain lions are almost silent when they move.**
Soft pads spread weight and absorb sound.

⚠ **Tornadoes can form inside forest fires.**
Rising heat twists air into "fire whirls."

⚠ **Rip currents pull you outward, not under.**
They're narrow channels of fast-moving water.

⚠ **Hailstones can contain hundreds of layers.**
Storms cycle them up and down repeatedly before dropping.

⚠ **Some beaches have "sleeper waves."**
Long-period ocean swells create sudden giant waves with no warning.

⚠ **Certain frogs freeze solid in winter and thaw alive.**
They replace water in their cells with natural antifreeze.

⚠ **Hot springs can turn deadly with one misplaced step.**
Thin crusts hide scalding water just inches below.

⚠ **Coyotes can jump almost straight up.**
They spring 6–7 feet to clear fences or pounce prey.

⚠ **A falling icicle can kill you.**
Sharp ice falling from height builds shocking speed.

⚠ **Desert winds can polish rocks smoother than water.**
Wind-driven sand acts like natural sandpaper.

⚠ **Sleet can fall in sunshine.**
Cold upper air layers freeze raindrops before they melt on the way down.

⚠ **Hypothermia can happen above 50°F.**
Wet clothes strip body heat extremely fast.

⚠ **Some cliffs create wind that pushes climbers away from the wall.**
Updrafts form when warm valley air rises.

⚠ **Black ice forms quickest under clear skies.**
Heat radiates away at night, freezing thin moisture.

⚠ **Snow avalanches can jump gaps.**
Momentum carries them across ravines.

⚠ **Bison can spin on a dime.**
They pivot faster than their size suggests.

⚠ **Heat mirages on roads bend light like water.**
Hot air near the surface refracts upward, creating mirror illusions.

⚠ **Tree wells around evergreens can swallow people.**
Loose snow collapses inward around the trunk.

⚠ **Lake turnover can choke out fish overnight.**
Deep, oxygen-poor water rises during seasonal mixing.

⚠ **Some scorpions glow under UV light.**
Chemicals in their exoskeleton react to ultraviolet rays.

⚠ **Falling rocks can bounce unpredictably.**
Irregular shapes cause chaotic ricochets.

⚠ **Canyons amplify sound strangely.**
Echo waves collide and distort direction.

⚠ **Mountain storms can drop temperature 40 degrees in minutes.**
Cold air pours downhill like a liquid.

⚠ **Freshwater sharks exist.**
Bull sharks tolerate low salinity and travel upriver.

⚠ **Ground can liquify during earthquakes.**
Sandy soil loses structure under vibration.

⚠ **Stagnant water can create its own mini ecosystem in days.**
Sunlight, bacteria, and nutrients spark explosive growth.

⚠ **Thunder can carry 20+ miles.**
Low-frequency sound waves travel far.

⚠ **Sandstorms can strip paint from cars.**
Fast-blowing particles act like abrasives.

⚠ **Frozen waterfalls can collapse without warning.**
Ice fractures internally as temperatures rise.

⚠ **Humidity can make air feel hotter than it is.**
Moist air blocks sweat evaporation.

⚠ **Shallow water can cut like glass in high winds.**
Choppy waves fling debris at speed.

⚠ **Large rock slabs can "surf" downhill on mud.**
Landslides lubricate the surface beneath.

⚠ **Pine needles can conduct lightning.**
Sap and moisture form natural pathways.

⚠ **Fog can disorient your sense of direction.**
Your brain loses visual "anchor points."

⚠ **Even small rivers can move cars.**
Water gains power exponentially with depth.

⚠ **Invisible CO_2 carpet clouds**
These ground-hugging gas layers seep from volcanic vents and can knock you unconscious before you feel anything.

⚠ **Snowpack "whumpfs" before collapsing**
That soft, muffled thud is an entire weak layer failing under your weight, often moments before a slab avalanche releases.

⚠ **Rogue waves in freshwater lakes**
Sudden pressure shifts and long-period winds can create towering waves that appear with zero warning.

⚠ **Desert-varnish bacteria on rocks**
The glossy black coating sometimes hosts extremophile microbes that thrive in brutal heat and UV exposure.

⚠ **Debris flows that run uphill**
High internal pressure and liquefied sediment can push a mudflow upward like moving concrete.

⚠ **Super-cooled rain that freezes on skin**
Droplets below 32°F remain liquid until they touch you, then flash-freeze into a rigid ice shell.

⚠ **Ground-crawling lightning current**
A single strike can spread laterally for dozens of feet, shocking everything in its path.

147

⚠ **Glacial meltwater temperature shocks**
Surges of subglacial water can drop a river's temperature by 30 degrees in seconds.

⚠ **Oxygen-thin pockets in deserts**
Extreme heat lowers air density enough to make breathing feel strangely difficult at ground level.

⚠ **Collapsed crust over wasp caverns**
A thin layer of dirt often hides massive underground nests that break open when stepped on.

⚠ **Midnight katabatic wind drops**
Cold mountain air can suddenly plunge downhill and shred tents even after a calm evening.

⚠ **Methane-charged forest floors**
Organic decay traps flammable gas that bursts upward when disturbed.

⚠ **Ice caves melting from the inside**
Warm airflow hollows out chambers first, leaving deceptively strong-looking surfaces ready to collapse.

⚠ **Silent falls of hollow trees**
Rot removes internal tension, making entire trunks topple without the warning crack.

⚠ **Flash-drought ignition zones**
Rapid moisture loss can turn vegetation into wildfire fuel in only a few days.

⚠ **Riverbanks with hidden undercuts**
Water erodes the soil beneath, leaving a fragile shell that collapses like a trapdoor.

⚠ **"Depth hoar" sugar snow layers**
Angular ice crystals form loose, ball-bearing-like layers that destabilize entire slopes.

⚠ **Cold pools in mountain basins**
Dense air sinks and settles overnight, dropping temperatures far below the surrounding terrain.

⚠ **Air blasts from rockfall**
Large boulders displace so much air that the pressure wave can knock a person down without direct impact.

⚠ **Tidal bore upriver waves**
Shifting tides push a rolling wall of water inland, overturning boats in seconds.

⚠ **Erupting mud volcanoes**
Buried pressure pockets can blow through flat ground and blast boiling mud skyward.

⚠ **Heat-pressurized exploding bark**
Sap inside trunks can rapidly boil, shooting bark outward like shrapnel.

⚠ **Salt-flat crust over deep brine**
Solid-looking surfaces conceal watery mud that swallows anything that breaks through.

⚠ **Frozen-lake distance distortions**
Flat, featureless ice removes depth cues and tricks your eyes into misjudging distance and direction.

⚠ **Atmospheric gravity waves near mountains**
These invisible air waves can create violent turbulence, even in perfectly clear skies.

WEIRD FACTS — DANGEROUS OUTDOORS

MYTHS – BUSTED
DANGEROUS OUTDOORS

MYTHS

Myth #1: "Animals attack out of aggression."
Most attacks happen because animals feel cornered, startled, or are protecting young.

Myth #2: "If you can see lightning, you're safe."
Lightning travels sideways for miles before striking.

Myth #3: "You can outrun a bear."
You can't — they hit 35 mph in seconds.

Myth #4: "Clear skies mean safe weather."
Storm cells can form behind mountains and hit without warning.

Myth #5: "Snakes chase people."
They flee — the "chasing" illusion is often terrain forcing you both along the same path.

Myth #6: "River water is safe if it looks clean."
Giardia, bacteria, and parasites need no discoloration.

Myth #7: "Heatstroke always gives warning signs."
It can become severe in minutes with no early symptoms.

Myth #8: "Animals won't enter campsites."
Food smells travel long distances.

Myth #9: "Snow is safe if it's deep."
Deep snow hides crevasses, tree wells, and thin ice.

Myth #10: "Cold kills faster than heat."
Heat kills more people annually worldwide.

Myth #11: "Only big predators are dangerous."
Deer, cows, and moose injure more people than predators combined.

Myth #12: "Quicksand pulls you under."
It holds you afloat — panic is what kills.

Myth #13: "You can see rip currents from shore."
Many are invisible in calm surf.

Myth #14: "You'll smell smoke before wildfire danger."
Fast, wind-driven fires outrun their own smell.

Myth #15: "Climbers rely on strength more than technique."
Technique determines survival — not muscle.

WEIRD FACTS!

Some cliffs hide 'gravity-loaded' boulders that can shift from a single footstep — stored tension snapping like a trap.

Cold-air avalanches can rush down mountains at night — invisible until they pick up dust and debris.

Entire forest floors can collapse into hidden lava tubes or old mining shafts with no warning.

Some lakes release pockets of deadly CO_2 — enough to suffocate everything nearby in seconds.

CH 9 — DANGEROUS OUTDOORS

MIND-BLOWN™ Cartoons

LEGENDS
DANGEROUS OUTDOORS

LEGENDS

The Vanishing Lake Lights — Glacier National Park

Backcountry campers have reported floating blue or silver lights drifting across remote alpine lakes long after dark. The lights skim low over the water, then shoot straight upward and disappear. Rangers call them "temperature inversion reflections," but longtime locals insist they're the spirits of lost travelers still searching for a way across the mountains.

The Black Whispers of Hatcher Pass — Alaska

On windless nights, hikers have described hearing whispered conversations carried across the valley — voices speaking in no known language. The sound often stops instantly when approached. Miners in the early 1900s claimed the pass was patrolled by "shadow talkers," spirits that guard hidden gold veins.

The Red Eyes of Linville Gorge — North Carolina

For nearly a century, nighttime climbers have reported two glowing red eyes staring at them from cliff edges or treetops, always motionless and always too high to belong to any normal animal. Wildlife officials dismiss them as reflections, but search-and-rescue teams quietly admit they've seen the same thing... and sometimes felt watched for miles.

The Singing Boulders of Death Valley

A few massive rocks in remote desert washes emit low, humming tones on certain nights — vibrations felt more than heard. Geologists attribute it to thermal contraction, but the tone carries too far and lasts too long. Shoshone stories describe them as "stones that remember," holding voices of ancestors who once crossed the desert.

The Phantom Fire Line — Yosemite Backcountry

Backpackers deep in the high country sometimes see a glowing orange band on the horizon, like a distant wildfire. But it never grows, never generates smoke, and vanishes the moment someone tries to get closer. Rangers suspect an extremely rare atmospheric refraction. Old Paiute legends call it the "Sky Line," a boundary between the living world and the spirit trails above it.

The Hollow Footsteps of Big Bend

Night hikers crossing desert flats have reported footsteps walking behind them — perfectly timed with their own, but delayed by a half beat. When they stop, the steps stop. When they run, the steps run. Search logs are full of similar accounts going back decades. Rangers blame shifting gravel. Locals say it's "the follower," a desert spirit that mimics travelers to see if they fear the dark.

The Shadow Elk of Rocky Mountain National Park

Hunters and backcountry skiers have described enormous elk-shaped shadows galloping across snowfields — with no physical elk casting them. The silhouettes move silently and leave no tracks. Biologists have no explanation for the optical illusion. Ute stories speak of "sky elk," spirits that run ahead of storms.

The Wailing Wind of Canyonlands
In certain slot canyons, gusts produce a haunting, humanlike wail —
but only after sunset. Visitors describe it starting as a low moan and
rising into a sharp cry. Airflow physics explains part of it, but many
hikers report hearing multiple "voices" layered together, sometimes
shifting locations as if following them.

The Staircase Lights of Mount Shasta
Backpackers have reported stacked bands of white light rising in the
night sky above a few ridges, forming what looks like glowing steps.
They flicker for a few seconds and vanish. Scientists cite rare ice
crystal refractions. Indigenous lore says they are "spirit ladders,"
pathways for sky beings traveling between realms.

MYTHS & LEGENDS!

MYTH: A dry canyon is safe.
FACT: Flash floods can originate 20+ miles away and arrive silently, with no rain in sight.

MYTH: Hypothermia requires freezing temps.
FACT: It can happen at 50°F — especially when wet or tired.

MYTH: You can escape danger by climbing trees.
FACT: Bears, cougars, and even wolves can climb faster than humans.

MYTH: Follow water to civilization.
FACT: Water often leads into cliffs, slot canyons, or waterfalls — trapping hikers.

MIND-BLOWN™ Cartoons

DID YOU KNOW?
DANGEROUS OUTDOORS

What animal kills the most people worldwide?
Mosquitoes (disease).

Which weather event causes the most U.S. deaths annually?
Heat waves.

What should you do if caught in a rip current?
Swim parallel to shore.

Which animal can detect your heartbeat from several feet away?
Sharks.

What color clothing attracts more insects?
Dark colors.

Which natural event can lift a lake?
Earthquakes.

Did you know sudden drops in barometric pressure at altitude can trigger strokes in otherwise healthy hikers?
It's one of the least-known high-mountain killers.

Did you know flash floods in slot canyons can outrun Olympic sprinters?
They often move 20–30 mph with zero warning.

Did you know dry lightning can strike miles from any visible storm?
Up to 10% of lightning events occur with no thunder at all.

Did you know desert sand can reach 160°F on hot days?
Hot enough to burn through thin shoe soles in under a minute.

Did you know more hikers die from cold-water shock than from hypothermia later on?
The initial gasp reflex alone can cause drowning.

Did you know high-altitude snowfields can hide crevasses beneath "false floors"?
The surface may hold your weight... until it doesn't.

Did you know wind on exposed ridges can surge from 10 mph to 70+ mph in a single gust?
Microbursts form instantly and without visible buildup.

Did you know pine trees can explode during wildfires?
Resin inside them superheats and expands into vapor, blowing the trunk apart.

Did you know volcanoes can produce deadly lahars centuries after they go dormant?
Heavy rainfall alone can reactivate old mudflow channels.

Did you know sneaker waves can be ten times larger than the waves before them?
They hit without warning and often never return victims.

Did you know some deserts form "death mirages"?
They mimic water but actually mark unstable cold-air sinkholes.

Did you know lightning bolts can rise upward from the ground before the visible strike comes down?
They're called upward leaders and can travel over a mile.

STORY MOMENT DANGEROUS OUTDOORS

The Thing in the Temperature Drop

I was hiking a remote ridge in the Uintas, where the trail fades and the forest feels older than the map suggests. Storms were forming far off, but the air around me was warm and still.

Then the temperature crashed — a sudden ten-degree plunge, no wind, no shadow. My breath fogged. In July. The forest went silent, even the insects. A narrow twenty-foot stretch ahead felt like a freezer, and the trees creaked under shifting pressure.

A low, vibrating hum rose — not mechanical, just wrong. I stepped back and the warmth returned; forward again and the cold slammed into me. Something flickered beside the trail: a freezing distortion, like heat-waves running backward. Pressure built in my ears, sharp and immediate.

The distortion slid a few inches... then vanished.
Warmth snapped back.

That's when I noticed the branches in that short section coated with **rime ice** — delicate frost that forms only in freezing fog, yet the air was bone dry. A perfect band of ice standing in summer air like a doorway.

I still don't know what I crossed — a rogue atmospheric collapse or something with no name yet. But when storms build now, the same pressure gathers behind my ears... like whatever brushed past me is waiting to return.

? QUIZ
DANGEROUS OUTDOORS
QUIZ

Multiple Choice

1. What makes rip currents dangerous?
   A. They drag swimmers underwater
   B. They pull swimmers outward fast
   C. They create whirlpools
   D. They shock the water

2. Why can avalanches reach extreme speeds?
   A. They contain trapped air
   B. They fall through air pockets
   C. They contain ice sheets
   D. Snow is slippery

3. Which animal injures more people than predators?
   A. Wolves
   B. Snakes
   C. Moose
   D. Bears

4. Why can mountains create sudden storms?
   A. They reflect sunlight
   B. They block humidity
   C. They lift warm air upward
   D. They cool the ground

5. What causes "booming dunes"?
   A. Wind whistling
   B. Sand grains vibrating
   C. Animals moving
   D. Earthquakes

Fill-in-the-Blank

1. Cold water steals heat _____ times faster than cold air.

2. Falling ice from heights builds surprising _____.

3. Desert temperatures drop fast because dry air can't hold _____.

True or False

1. Clear water is always safe to drink.

2. Lightning can strike from miles away.

3. Deep snow is always safe to walk on.

WEIRD FACTS!

"Some lakes can explode without warning — releasing enough trapped CO_2 to suffocate everything within miles."

"Mountain canyons can create wind tunnels where gusts exceed 100 mph — even on calm days."

"Before a lightning strike, your entire body can become electrically charged — a silent warning seconds before impact."

"Lightning can strike the ground miles away from the bolt — the ground current kills more people than lightning itself."

CH 9 — DANGEROUS OUTDOORS

MIND-BLOWN™ Cartoons

QUIZ ANSWERS
DANGEROUS OUTDOORS

Multiple Choice

1. **B**

2. **A**

3. **C**

4. **C**

5. **B**

Fill-in-the-Blank

1. **25**

2. **speed**

3. **heat**

True or False

1. **False**

2. **True**

3. **False**

10

MOUNTAINS, CAVES & CANYONS

WEIRD FACTS!

SOME MOUNTAIN CLIFFS ARE SO TALL THEY CREATE THEIR OWN WEATHER.

SOME MOUNTAIN CLIFFS ARE SO TALL THEY CREATE THEIR OWN WEATHER.

SOME CAVES ARE SO LARGE THEY CAN HOLD ENTIRE SKYSCRAPERS.

CANYON ROCK LAYERS CAN BE MILLIONS OF YEARS APART.

SOME UNDERGROUND RIVERS TRAVEL FOR MILES WITHOUT EVER SEEING SUNLIGHT.

CH 10 — MOUNTAINS, CAVES & CANYONS

MIND-BLOWN™ Cartoons

WEIRD & FUN FACTS MOUNTAINS, CAVES & CANYONS

MIND-BLOWN MOMENT

🏔 **Some mountains rise faster than fingernails grow,** because tectonic plates shove into each other with slow but unstoppable force.

🏔 **Caves sometimes "breathe" warm air in winter and cold air in summer,** as underground pressure forces air in and out like a giant set of lungs.

🏔 **Entire cave systems can collapse silently,** because the rock above dissolves or weakens long before humans ever notice cracks on the surface.

🏔 **Frozen waterfalls exist inside deep caves,** formed when dripping water meets temperatures cold enough to build ice sculptures taller than people.

🏔 **The Grand Canyon reveals nearly two billion years of Earth's history,** because erosion peeled it open layer by layer like Earth's longest time machine.

🏔 **Mountains can produce phantom shadows that stretch hundreds of miles,** caused by low-angle sunlight hitting sharply pointed peaks.

🏔 **Cave lakes can be so clear they seem invisible,** because mineral-rich water filters out particles that would normally cloud it.

🏔 **Some cliffs "buzz" during thunderstorms,** as lightning charges make minerals vibrate microscopically.

🏔 **There are mountains whose peaks never melt, even during heatwaves**, because thin high-altitude air can't hold warmth.

🏔 **Quartz-rich rocks inside canyons can spark blue flashes at night**, created when they crack under stress — a phenomenon called triboluminescence.

🏔 **A cave in Mexico grows crystals larger than buses**, because superheated mineral-rich water cooled extremely slowly.

🏔 **Some canyons create their own wind systems**, as warm air rises up the cliffs and cooler air rushes in to replace it.

🏔 **Mountains can cause rain to fall only on one side**, leaving deserts on the other — a result of moisture being squeezed out in a "rain shadow."

🏔 **Caves can preserve ancient air pockets**, trapped for thousands of years because no airflow reaches the sealed chambers.

🏔 **Canyon walls can develop dark "desert varnish"**, created by microbes slowly coating rock with manganese and iron over centuries.

🏔 **Massive pillars inside caves form when stalactites and stalagmites meet**, after tens of thousands of years of slow mineral deposits.

🏔 **Some mountain plants only bloom once every several decades**, responding to tiny changes in temperature or soil chemistry.

🏔 **Caves can create low-frequency hums humans can't hear**, generated by airflow or vibrating rock that animals detect easily.

🔺 **Entire river systems can vanish underground**, flowing through limestone tunnels before reappearing miles away.

🔺 **The tallest mountain in the solar system is on Mars**, and it's three times taller than Everest because Mars lacks Earth's strong gravity.

🔺 **Slot canyons form from violent flash floods**, with walls shaved smooth by water moving fast enough to carry boulders like ping-pong balls.

🔺 **Underground waterfalls can run for centuries**, fed by steady groundwater seeping through cracks from far above.

🔺 **Mountains can "glow" red at sunrise and sunset**, a phenomenon called alpenglow caused by indirect light scattering through the atmosphere.

🔺 **Caves often stay the same temperature year-round**, insulated from seasonal changes by thick layers of rock.

🔺 **Some canyons grow wider faster after fires**, because burnt soil absorbs water poorly, increasing rapid erosion.

🔺 **There are caves with rivers so strong they create standing waves**, formed when confined channels accelerate water like a pressure hose.

🔺 **Mountains create their own microclimates**, allowing wildly different plants to grow just a few hundred feet apart.

🔺 **Cave pearls form without any clam at all**, created when dripping water rolls mineral grains into perfectly round balls.

🔺 **Some rocks in canyon walls grow strange patterns**, caused by iron oxidation leaving trails that look like fossilized plants.

🔺 **Entire cave systems form from acidic rainwater**, which becomes corrosive as it mixes with carbon dioxide in soil.

🏔 **The Himalayas rose high enough to change global weather**, altering jet streams and monsoon patterns across continents.

🏔 **Stalactites can grow hollow tubes thinner than straws**, formed by capillary action pulling water along microscopic channels.

🏔 **Mountains can act like giant amplifiers**, bouncing sound between slopes so voices travel farther than expected.

🏔 **Some caves contain minerals that fluoresce neon colors**, glowing under ultraviolet light thanks to unusual chemical structures.

🏔 **Many mountain lakes sit in ancient volcanic craters**, filled long after eruptions left behind huge empty bowls.

🏔 **Flash floods can carve new canyon features overnight**, because water pressure increases exponentially in narrow spaces.

🏔 **Caves with flowing rivers often change shape every year**, as sediment cuts channels deeper or shifts rock fragments.

🏔 **Certain canyon rocks split into perfect hexagons**, created when lava cools evenly and contracts into geometric patterns.

🏔 **Some mountains make clouds that look like UFOs**, formed when stable, moist air flows over peaks in smooth, lens-shaped layers.

🏔 **Ice caves can form blue walls that seem to glow**, as thick ice absorbs warm colors and lets only blue wavelengths pass through.

🏔 **Deep caves contain "moonmilk," a soft mineral paste**, produced when bacteria break down rock into smooth, creamy powder.

165

🏔️ **Canyon walls can "echo" multiple times**, not from loudness but from narrow, twisting passages bouncing sound in sequence.

🏔️ **The Rockies are still rising today**, because crustal forces continue to push them upward even as erosion wears them down.

🏔️ **Caves near volcanoes can fill with poisonous gases**, released from deep underground and trapped in low, still air.

🏔️ **A mountain's summit can be warmer than its base under certain conditions**, when warm air flows upslope and sinks cold air downward.

🏔️ **Some caves grow delicate crystal fans that can shatter with a whisper**, because they formed in still, undisturbed pools.

🏔️ **Water flowing through canyon rocks can create natural music**, as different-sized holes whistle at specific pitches.

🏔️ **In rare cases, caves form entirely from lava tubes**, hollow corridors left behind when the outer layer of flowing lava cooled first.

🏔️ **Mountains can disturb migrating birds**, creating air currents that force flocks to change direction unexpectedly.

🏔️ **Certain canyons create optical illusions**, making water appear to run uphill due to tilted horizons and angled rock layers.

MYTHS – BUSTED
MOUNTAINS, CAVES & CANYONS

Myth #1: "Mountains are solid rock all the way through."
Fact: Many contain hollow chambers, ancient lava tubes, unstable fault zones, and entire cave systems threaded through them.

Myth #2: "Caves are pitch-black, silent, and empty."
Fact: Many pulse with dripping water, unseen airflow, mineral pops, bats, insects, and even unique life-forms found nowhere else on Earth.

Myth #3: "Canyon walls never move."
Fact: Micro-quakes, freeze–thaw cycles, and flash-flood erosion constantly shift rock layers — sometimes triggering full wall collapses.

Myth #4: "High altitude always means colder temperatures."
Fact: Temperature inversions can flip the script, making mountaintops warmer than valleys trapped under cold, dense air.

Myth #5: "Stalactites and stalagmites grow the same way everywhere."
Fact: Their shape depends on mineral chemistry, airflow patterns, humidity, and even bacteria that help create crystal structures.

Myth #6: "Canyons take millions of years to form."
Fact: Some side canyons appear shockingly fast — a single extreme flash flood can carve new channels in hours.

Myth #7: "All cave systems connect underground."
Fact: Most don't — their passages form from unique fractures,

167

dissolving rock in isolated pockets rather than one big tunnel network.

Myth #8: "Rocks don't make sound unless they're falling."
Fact: Canyon walls and mountain cliffs can hum, whistle, and vibrate due to temperature stress, mineral expansion, or resonating winds.

Myth #9: "Mountain animals are harmless unless provoked."
Fact: Many appear calm because they're conserving energy — sudden movements or surprise encounters can trigger explosive reactions.

Myth #10: "You can't get lost in a canyon; you just follow the walls."
Fact: Maze-like slot systems, false turns, echoing passages, and rising floodwaters have trapped countless hikers.

MYTHS & LEGENDS!

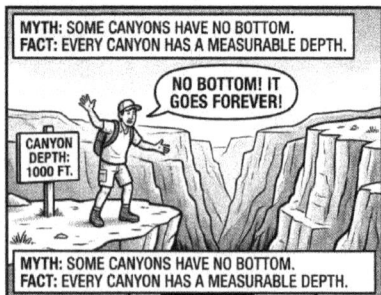

MYTH: MOUNTAINS HIDE SECRET LOST CITIES.
FACT: NO CITIES HAVE EVER BEEN FOUND INSIDE THEM.

MYTH: CAVE SHADOWS ARE GHOSTS.
FACT: THEY'RE CAUSED BY UNEVEN ROCK AND LIGHT.

MYTH: SOME CANYONS HAVE NO BOTTOM.
FACT: EVERY CANYON HAS A MEASURABLE DEPTH.

MYTH: MOUNTAIN FACES ARE CARVED BY ANY PEOPLE.
FACT: THEY'RE NATURAL EROSION PATTERNS.

MYTH: SOME CANYONS HAVE NO BOTTOM.
FACT: EVERY CANYON HAS A MEASURABLE DEPTH.

MYTH: MOUNTAIN FACES ARE CARVED BY ANCIENT PEOPLE.
FACT: THEY'RE NATURAL EROSION PATTERNS.

Ch 10 — MOUNTAINS, CAVES & CANYONS

MIND-BLOWN™ Cartoons

LEGENDS
MOUNTAINS, CAVES & CANYONS

LEGENDS

The Breathing Canyon — Cedar Mesa, Utah

Hikers deep in remote side canyons report the walls expanding and contracting with a slow, steady rhythm, as if the rock itself is breathing. Dust lifts in tiny pulses, and warm air cycles in and out of cracks with a heartbeat-like pattern. Geologists blame trapped pressure waves, but local guides say the canyon inhales travelers it does not intend to let back out.

The Echo That Answers Wrong — Mammoth Cave, Kentucky

Certain chambers return echoes that alter the words shouted into them. Phrases come back shorter, broken, or whispered in a stranger's voice. Acoustic tests can't replicate it, and veteran guides refuse to raise their voices there, claiming the cave returns echoes of people it has already claimed.

The Shadow Crossing — Grand Teton National Park

Climbers have seen a tall, upright shadow glide across opposite rock faces, stepping over ledges no human could reach. It moves steadily and disappears the moment someone looks directly at it. Minutes later, ropes sometimes swing from an unseen force, as if something just passed them heading down.

The Whispering Shaft — Carlsbad Caverns, New Mexico

In a narrow vertical shaft, explorers hear faint whispers when the lights are off. The voices rise from the darkness in multiple languages—fragments of prayers, names, and final pleas. Airflow sensors show no movement. Old cavers say the shaft collects last words and repeats them to warn new visitors.

The Blue Walker of Mount Shasta — California
Campers on the eastern slopes have reported a tall, bluish figure walking the ridgeline after midnight. It appears elongated and translucent, taking slow, deliberate strides before vanishing. Some call it an atmospheric mirage; others insist it is a mountain guardian that appears only on the nights someone below will not return.

The Canyon of Vanishing Footprints — Zion Backcountry, Utah
Fresh boot prints in wet sand have been seen erasing themselves from heel to toe within minutes, with no flowing water and stable humidity. Rangers blame collapsing subsurface moisture layers, but local lore says the canyon removes the footprints of people it has already "marked."

The Lantern Line — Marble Canyon, Arizona
River runners sometimes spot a row of faint yellow lights moving in single file along sheer canyon walls far above any known trail. The lights drift, pause, and fade one by one. No camps or climbers are ever found. Older families say the canyon still holds the ghost herds and their night drovers.

The Gate of Cold Air — Dolomites, Italy
Mountaineers describe a narrow notch between two limestone towers where the temperature plunges instantly, even under full

sun. Frost forms on rock in seconds, then disappears as soon as you step out. Meteorologists cannot explain such a precise microclimate. Legends say it is a passing point for mountain spirits.

The Red Lake Under the Mountain — Karst Caves, Slovenia
Divers in a submerged chamber have seen a pool glow dark red, pulsing like a heartbeat before the color drains away. Water tests show nothing unusual. Locals quietly say the mountain is a sleeping being, and the pool reflects its dreams.

The Ridge of Frozen Sound — Canadian Rockies
Certain ridges mute all noise in winter. Footsteps, breathing, and even shouted words vanish a few inches from the mouth. Recordings capture only static hissing. Atmospheric science offers partial explanations, but Indigenous stories describe these places as crossings into a realm where sound does not exist.

The Moving Pit — Mexican Karst Plateau
Cavers have documented a deep sinkhole whose precise location appears to change between expeditions. The same dimensions and rock structure reappear hundreds of meters away. Satellite images remain unchanged. Locals believe the earth shifts dangerous paths to block some travelers and swallow others.

The Canyon Choir — Fiordland, New Zealand
Kayakers hear layered, harmonic singing drifting along narrow cliff channels on windless days. The patterns are too structured to be random. Acoustic analysis shows repeating sequences that resemble a composed melody. Māori tradition holds that ancestral spirits sing to guide—or warn—those passing through.

The Vanishing Bridge of Skye — Scotland

Hikers sometimes see a slender stone arch spanning a gorge, weathered and covered in lichen, only for it to recede as they approach. By the time they reach the edge, the arch is gone. Locals say the bridge appears only for those who are not meant to cross it.

The Cavern of Swapped Time — Undisclosed Alpine Cave

Explorers report spending what feels like a full night underground, only to emerge and find that almost no time has passed. Watches and gear logs match outside time perfectly. Some claim the cave trades empty hours for real ones, keeping the difference for itself.

The Firefall That Never Was — Hidden Cirque, Himalaya

Climbers have witnessed an orange, waterfall-like glow pouring down a cliff at twilight in a place with no watercourse or base camp above. When reached, the rock is cold and featureless. Sherpa legends say certain cliffs flare with light when a new event is being written into the mountain's story.

DID YOU KNOW?
MOUNTAINS, CAVES & CANYONS

Did you know some mountain peaks generate their own static-electric "halo" that can lift hair and make ice axes hum before a lightning strike?
This phenomenon, called a corona discharge, can happen even without visible storm clouds.

Did you know deep caves often contain air layers with different oxygen levels stacked like invisible strata?
Climbers can pass from breathable air into low-oxygen pockets in a single step.

Did you know canyon walls can act like acoustic lenses and bend sound so sharply that someone 300 feet away can sound inches behind you?
This effect has misled search-and-rescue teams for decades.

Did you know certain limestone caverns produce natural radiation spikes strong enough to disrupt watches and cameras?
Uranium-bearing rock seams can concentrate in unpredictable pockets.

Did you know mountain waves in the upper atmosphere can overturn commercial aircraft if pilots hit the wrong rotor zone?
These invisible standing waves can extend 30,000 feet high.

Did you know some canyons experience "temperature waterfalls," where cold air drops like liquid and flows downhill as a visible wave?
This dense-air cascade can disorient hikers and animals.

Did you know cave ceilings can grow bacteria that produce faint, cold light when disturbed?
This bioluminescence, often mistaken for ghost lights, appears only in untouched chambers.

Did you know granite mountain ranges can resonate during distant earthquakes like massive tuning forks?
The vibrations travel through bedrock and can last minutes after the quake stops.

Did you know explorers have recorded sudden pressure drops in deep caves equivalent to standing at 10,000 feet of altitude?
Rapid shifts can cause dizziness, vertigo, and tunnel vision without warning.

Did you know some canyon floors hide "dry quicksand," formed when ultra-fine dust traps air like a spring?
Stepping on it can drop a hiker knee-deep instantly.

Did you know mountain summits can throw light upward at night, creating faint vertical beams called "ghost pillars"?
They form when ice crystals align in thin high-altitude air.

Did you know certain cave systems have wind gusts strong enough to blow out headlamps — caused entirely by remote chambers changing temperature?
Airflow reversals can exceed 40 mph.

Did you know mountaineers have reported smelling sulfur hours before volcanic vents show activity?

Some gas escapes through microfractures long before seismic instruments detect change.

Did you know canyon rock can store heat so efficiently that nighttime temperatures rise instead of fall?
Some desert canyons warm after sunset as the stone releases trapped solar energy.

Did you know several major cave systems still generate unexplained low-frequency "drumming" noises picked up on seismic equipment?
The source remains unknown — not water, not wind, not wildlife.

id you know some mountain ridges create invisible "gravity pockets" where objects fall slightly sideways instead of straight down?
The effect comes from micro-variations in local gravitational pull caused by dense mineral deposits.

Did you know certain deep caves produce sudden wind blasts that appear out of still air, with no tunnels behind them?
These "orphan gusts" are powerful enough to knock gear over and remain unexplained by airflow models.

Did you know canyon thunderstorms can create upward lightning strikes that originate from the ground and climb skyward like a branching tree?
These bolts can stretch a mile high before the main discharge follows.

Did you know some high-altitude cliff faces emit faint radio waves detectable on handheld receivers?
The signals match no known broadcast and are believed to come from piezoelectric stress in the rock.

175

STORY MOMENT
MOUNTAINS, CAVES & CANYONS

STORY
MOMENT

The Ledge That Listened

The approach trail was already thin, but the ledge was worse — a narrow stone ribbon halfway up a canyon wall in the Four Corners backcountry. No cell service, no cairns, just sandstone and silence. I'd followed rumors of an unmapped alcove with ancient markings. Most people shrugged it off as hiker legend. That should've been my first warning.

Halfway across the ledge, the air changed.
Not colder — *heavier*.
Like someone pressed a hand against the atmosphere itself.

I stopped moving. The canyon below was dead quiet, no wind at all. Then I heard something I still can't explain: a faint tapping coming from the rock behind me. Slow, deliberate. Three taps... a pause... then two more. Not an animal. Not falling debris. It was too measured.

I turned, but the stone was bare. Smooth.
The tapping stopped.

I kept moving.

Another ten feet along the ledge, something whispered — a soft, sliding sound, like a breath being pulled through narrow cracks. The kind of sound that makes the hair on your arms react before your brain does.

Then came the voice.

(continued...)

Not a word. Not a language.
Just a low, drawn-out sound that rose from the stone itself, vibrating through my boots. A tone that felt like it wasn't meant for human ears. My chest tightened. My vision pulsed at the edges. It felt like the canyon was warning me — or studying me.

Instinct said leave.
Curiosity said two more steps.

I took one.

Immediately the ledge beneath me trembled — a subtle shiver running through the rock. Loose sand skittered toward the drop as if gravity had tilted. I froze, palms flat against the wall.

Then the whisper returned — closer, inside the rock, almost beneath my hand. A pressure built behind my ears, sharp enough to blur my thoughts. And then I felt it: the faintest rhythmic pulse through the stone, like something deep inside the canyon was... listening. And responding.

I backed away slowly, step by step, never taking my hand from the wall until I reached safer ground. The moment my boots hit solid trail, the pulse stopped. The whispers cut off. The air lightened, as if whatever was paying attention decided I wasn't worth the effort.

I never found that alcove.
I never went back to that ledge.
But sometimes, when I hike near canyon walls, I feel that same pressure behind my ears — like the stone is waiting for me to make one more step in the wrong direction.

Waiting to listen again.

QUIZ
MOUNTAINS, CAVES & CANYONS

QUIZ

1. True or False: A mountain can shrink even while tectonic forces are pushing it upward.

2. Which process can create a brand-new side canyon in a single afternoon?
A) Ice creep
B) Flash flooding
C) Seismic settling
D) Wind abrasion

3. Stalactites develop unique shapes depending on changes in _____.
A) Mineral chemistry and airflow
B) Moon cycles
C) Sunlight angles
D) Magnetic fields

4. A U-shaped valley is evidence of which past event?
A) Volcanic eruption
B) Glacial movement
C) Earthquake uplift
D) Rockfall erosion

5. What causes some mountain lakes to appear neon-turquoise even under cloudy skies?
A) Algae colonies
B) Suspended rock flour
C) Solar reflection
D) Radioactive minerals

6. True or False: Some caves maintain such stable temperatures that seasonal outside weather has almost zero influence.

7. Which phenomenon explains why deep canyons can appear to glow red at sunrise or sunset?
A) Atmospheric refraction
B) Alpenglow
C) Radiant inversion
D) Canyon bloom

8. Which factor causes canyon walls to break, shear, or collapse unexpectedly?
A) Pressure from groundwater freezing in cracks
B) Random chance
C) Magnetic resonance
D) Lunar tides

9. An underground cavern suddenly "breathing" outward with warm air is usually caused by _____.
A) Shifting barometric pressure between cave chambers and the surface
B) Volcanic lava movement
C) Chemical heating of rock
D) Moonlight reflecting underground

10. A cave filled with perfectly clear water that looks bottomless is most likely due to:
A) Absolute purity
B) Suspended silica
C) Calcite-rich water that hides optical depth
D) Microbial fluorescence

QUIZ ANSWERS
MOUNTAINS, CAVES & CANYONS

1. **True**

2. **B — Flash flooding**

3. **A — Mineral chemistry and airflow**

4. **B — Glacial movement**

5. **B — Suspended rock flour**

6. **True**

7. **B — Alpenglow**

8. **A — Pressure from groundwater freezing in cracks**

9. **A — Shifting barometric pressure between cave chambers and the surface**

10. **C — Calcite-rich water that hides optical depth**

11

STARS & SPACE

WEIRD FACTS!

Some stars you see in the night sky already died thousands of years ago — their light is only reaching us now.

The Milky Way isn't a cloud — it's the combined light of 100+ billion stars.

The largest known stars are so big our entire solar system could fit inside them.

SUN

Earth's atmosphere extends farther than the Moon's orbit — just extremely thin.

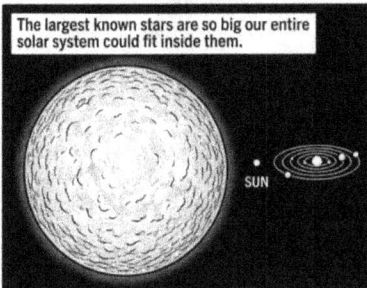

Ch 11 — SKY, STARS & SPACE

MIND-BLOWN™ Cartoons

WEIRD & FUN FACTS
STARS & SPACE

MIND-BLOWN MOMENT

- **The sky's blue color isn't the default — it's a side effect of scattering.**
  Short wavelengths like blue bounce off air molecules more easily, painting the daytime sky in colors our eyes interpret as blue.

- **Stars don't twinkle in space at all.**
  They only shimmer from Earth because shifting pockets of warm and cold air bend their light unpredictably.

- **Sunsets are more vivid after volcanic eruptions.**
  Tiny ash particles scatter long-wavelength red light, making the sky look like it's on fire for months.

- **Noctilucent clouds glow long after sunset.**
  They form so high in the mesosphere that they still catch sunlight even when the ground is in darkness.

- **Airglow makes the night sky shimmer green.**
  Atoms in the upper atmosphere release energy absorbed from daytime sunlight, creating faint nighttime glows.

- **The Milky Way is brightest in winter for northern observers.**
  We're looking toward a denser arm of our galaxy packed with stars, gas clouds, and dust lanes.

- **Venus is bright enough to cast a shadow on Earth.**
  Its thick clouds reflect sunlight so efficiently that it becomes a natural lantern in dark conditions.

- **Some meteors explode with a flash called a bolide.**
  Extreme pressure causes them to break apart mid-air, releasing shockwaves of light.

- **Auroras can crackle or hiss in extreme cold.**
  Electrical discharges near the ground interact with frigid, dry air to create faint, static-like sounds.
- **Most shooting stars are smaller than a grain of rice.**
  Their speed — not size — creates the dramatic streak of light.
- **The upper atmosphere vibrates with giant waves.**
  Gravity waves ripple like ocean swells, distorting stars and the aurora as they move.
- **Red sprites flash above thunderstorms.**
  These giant electrical discharges fire upward, not downward, reaching the edge of space.
- **The darkest nights on Earth aren't pitch-black.**
  Airglow, starlight, zodiacal dust, and distant city light combine to give the sky a faint sheen.
- **The sun emits neutrinos that pass through you by the trillions.**
  They almost never interact with matter, making them ghost-like particles streaming straight through Earth.
- **Stars appear different colors because of temperature**, not distance.
  Blue stars are hotter; red stars are cooler.
- **Clouds can weigh millions of pounds.**
  Their droplets are tiny enough that rising air keeps them aloft despite their mass.
- **Halos form around the sun when light hits hexagonal ice crystals.**
  The crystals act like prisms, bending light into perfect rings.
- **Some nights reveal "zodiacal light," a pale cone in the west.**
  It's sunlight reflecting off dust from ancient comets.
- **Satellites flare when the sun hits their panels just right.**
  For a second, they shine brighter than any star.

- **Planets don't twinkle like stars.**
  They're closer and appear as larger discs, so atmospheric turbulence affects them less.

- **Temperature inversions can make distant cities float.**
  Light bends through warm and cold layers to create mirage-like sky cities.

- **Lightning bolts can stretch more than 400 miles.**
  Massive supercell storms can sustain electrical channels across entire states.

- **Polar stratospheric clouds glow like neon curtains.**
  Their ice crystals are so reflective they shimmer in bright pinks and blues.

- **The night sky can pulse subtly in brightness.**
  Air pressure waves from storms travel hundreds of miles and ripple the upper atmosphere.

- **You can sometimes see your own shadow cast by starlight alone.**
  Under perfect dark-sky conditions, the combined light of billions of stars becomes measurable.

- **Meteor showers repeat yearly because Earth crosses the same debris streams.**
  Each pass through a comet's trail ignites a burst of tiny meteors.

- **Clouds sometimes appear iridescent.**
  When water droplets are uniform in size, they diffract sunlight into rainbow colors.

- **The sun's light takes eight minutes to reach Earth.**
  If the sun disappeared, we wouldn't know immediately.

- **Some stars we see are already gone.**
  Their light left long before the star died, making the night sky a time machine.

- **The upper atmosphere becomes electrically charged during solar storms.**
  This disrupts radio signals and creates intense aurora activity.

- **A full moon looks larger near the horizon due to brain trickery.**
  The "moon illusion" comes from comparing it to objects like trees or buildings.
- **Cloud shadows in the sky can appear disconnected from the clouds themselves.**
  The angle of sunlight creates floating dark shapes that confuse depth perception.
- **Airplanes sometimes leave rainbow contrails.**
  Ice crystals in exhaust plume diffract sunlight into pastel colors.
- **The brightest star you can see is Sirius**, not Polaris.
  Its intense blue-white light outshines everything except the moon and planets.
- **Sunstorms can compress Earth's magnetic field.**
  When strong enough, they push auroras farther south than normal.
- **Some auroras appear red instead of green.**
  Different gases glow at different altitudes, with oxygen producing red emissions high above.
- **Stars spin extremely fast.**
  Some rotate hundreds of times per second — fast enough to flatten at the poles.
- **Moon halos predict incoming storms.**
  High cirrus clouds carrying ice crystals often arrive before major weather systems.
- **A meteor entering at a shallow angle can skip like a stone.**
  Instead of burning up instantly, it can skim the upper atmosphere and keep going.
- **Sunsets appear redder during fire season.**
  Smoke particles scatter blue light away, leaving reds to dominate.

- **Night-shining clouds form only during summer.**
  Water vapor rises unusually high and freezes into microscopic ice crystals.
- **Comets grow enormous tails when close to the sun.**
  Solar radiation vaporizes their surface, blowing dust into glowing streaks.
- **Stars can appear twice in one night due to refraction.**
  Near the horizon, their light bends so strongly that they pop up earlier than they "should."
- **A "false dawn" can appear before sunrise.**
  Zodiacal dust reflects sunlight long before the sun reaches the horizon.
- **The sun's corona is hotter than its surface.**
  Magnetic waves transfer energy upward, superheating the outer layer.

WEIRD FACTS!

At 60,000 feet the sky turns black, even in daytime — you're almost in space.

Gravity can warp light itself — a black hole can act like a cosmic magnifying glass.

Earth doesn't spin smoothly — it wobbles like a top, shifting our pole position over time.

Stars only 'twinkle' because of Earth's atmosphere — in space they shine perfectly steady.

CH 11 — SKY, STARS & SPACE

MIND-BLOWN™ Cartoons

MYTHS – BUSTED
STARS & SPACE

MYTHS

Myth #1: "Stars twinkle because they're tiny."
Fact: Turbulent air bends their light, making them shimmer.

Myth #2: "A red sky at night always predicts good weather."
Fact: It only applies when specific wind and pressure patterns are present.

Myth #3: "Shooting stars are falling stars."
Fact: They're meteoroids burning at thousands of degrees.

Myth #4: "The North Star is the brightest."
Fact: Polaris is helpful for navigation, not brightness.

Myth #5: "Clouds are weightless."
Fact: They can weigh millions of pounds.

Myth #6: "Thunder needs nearby lightning."
Fact: Lightning far beyond the horizon still produces thunder — you just can't hear it.

Myth #7: "Rainbows are physical objects."
Fact: A rainbow is an angle of light you can't ever reach.

Myth #8: "Constellations look the same everywhere."
Fact: Hemisphere, season, and latitude all reshape the sky.

Myth #9: "Dark skies mean no light pollution."
Fact: You may not see the long-wavelength glow, but sensors do.

Myth #10: "Auroras only happen near the poles."
Fact: Strong storms send them far toward the equator.

Myth #11: "Stars stay still in the sky."
Fact: Many stars move so fast they change position over a human lifetime — some by entire moon-widths.

Myth #12: "Meteor showers come from random debris."
Fact: Each major shower is leftover dust from a specific comet's orbit — Earth literally plows through its trail.

Myth #13: "Space is completely dark."
Fact: Even the deepest voids contain faint background glow from ancient starlight and cosmic radiation.

Myth #14: "The North Star is the brightest star."
Fact: It only appears important because it sits almost perfectly on Earth's rotational axis — dozens of stars outshine it.

Myth #15: "Auroras only happen near the ground."
Fact: They can form over 600 miles high, shifting color depending on which atmospheric layer gets hit.

Myth #16: "All planets orbit in perfect circles."
Fact: Many orbits are stretched so far they resemble elongated teardrops, sending planets from frozen darkness to scorching heat.

Myth #17: "Comets glow because of fire."
Fact: Their brightness comes from sunlight slamming into dust and gas, creating an electric-like fluorescence.

Myth #18: "The sky is blue because space is blue."
Fact: Earth's air molecules scatter short wavelengths, turning the whole atmosphere into a giant light filter.

LEGENDS
STARS & SPACE

LEGENDS

The Whistling Aurora — Northern Canada & Alaska
For centuries, Inuit and First Nations communities have described the aurora making faint crackling or whistling sounds. Modern science confirms these reports: under rare conditions, geomagnetic activity can trigger audible static-like noises close to the ground. Elders believed the aurora carried the voices of ancestors — and that whistling back invited them to come closer.

The Hessdalen Lights — Norway
In a remote valley, glowing orbs of light appear in the sky, drifting, hovering, or streaking off at high speed. The phenomenon has been recorded for decades, with hundreds of eyewitness accounts and multiple scientific expeditions. The lights are real — but no single explanation fully fits their behavior. Locals long believed the lights were warnings from mountain spirits guarding the valley.

The Marfa Mystery Lights — Texas
Since the late 1800s, people have seen bright, floating balls of light appearing over the desert scrub. They split, merge, dance, or fade without a sound. Some scientists point to temperature inversions; others disagree. Early ranchers said the lights were the ghosts of Apache scouts watching from a distance.

The Brown Mountain Lights — North Carolina
For over a century, hikers, hunters, and rangers have reported

glowing spheres rising from the forest or floating along ridgelines. The lights appear in multiple colors, sometimes pulsing or drifting horizontally. Cherokee stories say these are the souls of fallen warriors searching for their lost families.

The Phoenix "Black Triangle" Sightings — Arizona
During the famous 1997 Phoenix Lights event, many witnesses described a massive, silent triangular shape that blocked out stars as it passed. The object's dark form was more disturbing than the lights themselves. Some residents believed it was a sky-being from Hopi creation stories, returning to observe the desert.

The Green Flash at Sunset — World Coasts
Sailors for centuries told tales of a brief green flame bursting above the horizon at sunset. The flash is real — a rare optical refraction when atmospheric layers bend sunlight. Early mariners believed seeing it meant the watcher had glimpsed the soul of the ocean for a split second.

The "Morning Glory" Cloud — Queensland, Australia
In remote regions of the Gulf of Carpentaria, enormous rolling tube-shaped clouds form that can stretch over 600 miles. They move with eerie smoothness, turning the sky into a giant rotating cylinder. Indigenous lore speaks of sky-serpents traveling between seasons, using the cloud as their path.

The Naga Fireballs — Mekong River, Thailand & Laos
Each year at the end of Buddhist Lent, glowing red orbs rise straight from the river and ascend into the night sky. Thousands witness them annually. Scientists debate whether the lights are gas bubbles,

plasma, or something else entirely. Locals insist they are the breath of the Naga — a massive serpent said to live beneath the river and the stars.

The Fata Morgana Sky Mirage — Polar & Desert Regions
This extreme type of mirage can make distant mountains float in the sky, turn ships into hovering castles, or create upside-down horizons. Before science understood refraction, explorers believed they were seeing entire ghost cities in the clouds. Inuit oral history calls them glimpses of "the land that exists above this land."

The "Sky Trumpets" Phenomenon — Worldwide
For decades, people around the world have recorded eerie trumpet-like sounds echoing from the sky, sometimes lasting minutes. No single explanation has been confirmed. Some suggest atmospheric ducting; others point to Earth's natural resonances. In multiple cultures, these were believed to be warnings from sky spirits or omens of coming change.

The Min Min Lights — Outback Australia
These mysterious lights follow travelers, hover at a distance, and change direction instantly. Reports go back to Aboriginal Dreamtime stories and early ranching journals. Scientists have theories, but none fully match the behavior. Elders said the lights were the souls of ancestors guiding the living — or watching them.

The Northern Sky Spiral — Norway, 2009
Thousands witnessed a glowing blue spiral expanding across the sky, lasting nearly two minutes. It was later attributed to a failed missile, but many locals still believe it was a modern version of

ancient sky omens. Sámi traditions speak of spirals appearing when the sky "opens to release a message."

The St. Elmo's Fire Glow — Mountain Peaks Worldwide
Climbers throughout history have seen climbing poles, tents, ice-axes, and ridgelines glow blue or violet just before storms. The plasma discharge is real — a build-up of electrical charge in thin air. For centuries, mountaineers considered it a sign the mountain deities were passing judgment on who could continue.

The Transient Lunar Phenomena — Moon, Hundreds of Reports
Since the 1600s, astronomers have recorded unexplained flashes, glows, color changes, and mist-like hazes on the moon's surface. Many modern observations remain unverified. Early sky-watchers believed these were signs of lunar spirits or the moon "breathing" through hidden vents.

The Zodiacal Light — Deserts & High Mountains
In extremely dark places, a massive pyramid-shaped glow appears stretching upward before dawn or after dusk — sunlight reflecting off ancient dust left over from early solar system formation. Cultures from Egypt to the Andes believed it was a celestial staircase used by gods to travel between heaven and earth.

DID YOU KNOW?
STARS & SPACE

Did you know Earth's atmosphere creates faint ultraviolet and infrared glows all the time — even on moonless nights?
This "airglow" covers the entire planet and is bright enough to cast shadows in extremely dark places.

Did you know some meteors explode with the force of nuclear weapons — completely unnoticed because they detonate high above the atmosphere?
These "airbursts" can equal tens of kilotons of energy, with only infrasound sensors detecting them.

Did you know cosmic rays constantly hit your body — and occasionally one particle can pass through your brain with enough energy to disrupt a single neuron?
This rare phenomenon, called a "cosmic-ray brain event," has been recorded in sensitive equipment worn by astronauts.

Did you know astronauts have reported seeing flashes of light with their eyes closed?
Cosmic radiation interacts with the retina, creating spontaneous "light streaks" in total darkness.

Did you know some stars pulse in size and brightness so dramatically that ancient cultures used them as seasonal clocks?
Mira, a red giant, brightens by 1,600% every 332 days — visible changes that people tracked long before telescopes existed.

Did you know the night sky has "cold spots" where microwave background radiation dips lower than expected — and physicists still don't fully know why?
The largest one, the CMB Cold Spot, is so unusual it suggests either a cosmic void or unknown physics at play.

Did you know thunder and meteor trails can interact — creating brief ionized channels that glow like faint, floating ribbons in the upper atmosphere?
These rare events are visible only from aircraft or high mountains during specific storms.

Did you know the color of starlight changes with altitude — so a star viewed from a high peak can look completely different than the same star at sea level?
Thin atmosphere dramatically reduces scattering, revealing colors hidden in the lowlands.

Did you know Earth passes through multiple streams of ancient comet debris each year — and some of those streams predate human civilization by millennia?
Meteor showers like the Taurids come from debris older than recorded history.

Did you know that faint, ghostlike "noctilucent clouds" form at the edge of space and shine long after sunset — but only under extremely specific atmospheric conditions?
They're the rarest clouds on Earth, seen mostly from high latitudes and created from ice crystals in the mesosphere.

MYTHS & LEGENDS!

MYTH: The Moon's "dark side" is always dark.
FACT: It gets sunlight — we just never see that hemisphere from Earth.

MYTH: Planet alignments trigger earthquakes.
FACT: Their gravity is too weak to matter.

MYTH: Space is completely empty.
FACT: It's filled with particles, radiation, and even rogue planets.

MYTH: Shooting stars are stars.
FACT: They're tiny bits of rock burning up in our atmosphere.

MYTH: Shooting stars stars.
FACT: They're tiny bits of rock burning up in our atmosphere.

MIND-BLOWN™ Cartoons

195

STORY MOMENT
STARS & SPACE

The Visitor Above the Canyon

I was trying to reach a canyon overlook before dark when I noticed a single bright light gliding across the sky — not fast like a satellite, not drifting like a plane. It simply moved... then paused high above me. Too high for aircraft, too steady for anything with wings.

Its color shifted with the fading sunset: white, then green, then a soft orange. It slid sideways, drawing an arc no normal flight path could make. I sat on the rock and watched, feeling more curious than uneasy.

After a minute, the canyon below flashed briefly, as if from a silent camera. When I looked up again, the single light had become two — faint, paired, hovering together. They drifted toward each other and merged, pulsing gently in a slow, steady rhythm.

The pulse felt like a quiet acknowledgment, not a warning.

Then the light dimmed, rose straight upward, and shrank into the deepening sky until it vanished. No sound. No trail. Just a smooth departure.

I waited awhile, hoping it might return. The stars eventually took over, steady and familiar. But I kept thinking about that moment — how whatever it was didn't seem threatening or curious in a human way.

More like something simply passing through...
and noticing someone who happened to be looking up.

QUIZ
STARS & SPACE
QUIZ QUIZ

1. True or False: Stars near the horizon appear redder because their light passes through more atmosphere.

2. Which phenomenon creates bright "false suns" during cold weather?
A) Sun mirrors
B) Halo arcs
C) Parhelia (sundogs)
D) Thermal refraction

3. Noctilucent clouds form in which atmospheric layer?
A) Troposphere
B) Mesosphere
C) Stratosphere
D) Thermosphere

4. The faint, glowing green band seen on dark nights is called _____.
A) Sky bloom
B) Airglow
C) Polar wash
D) Lumen drift

5. True or False: Aurora sounds have never been recorded scientifically.

6. Which planet can cast a visible shadow on Earth in perfect darkness?

A) Mars
B) Venus
C) Jupiter
D) Saturn

7. Annual meteor showers occur because:

A) Lunar tides intensify atmospheric drag
B) Earth passes through comet debris
C) Ice crystals reflect starlight
D) Solar wind pushes meteors inward

8. What fast-moving upper-atmospheric wind band dramatically affects flight times?

9. Stars "twinkle" primarily because of _____.

A) Their internal explosions
B) Atmospheric turbulence
C) Changing magnetic fields
D) Solar wind distortion

10. True or False: The Milky Way appears faint because it contains only a few thousand stars.

'In space nobody can hear you scream... except Mission Control, who replays it forever.'

'Astronaut Rule #14: Never admit you touched anything labeled "calibrated."'

'You know you've been in space too long when Earth starts looking like an ex.'

Zero-G is fun... until someone sneezes.

Even the universe stalls at 99%.

You know the mission's going badly when Houston starts with "Funny story..."

Q: What is a spaceman's favorite chocolate?
A: A Marsbar!

Q: Why did the sun go to school?
A: To get brighter!

Q: How do you know when the moon has enough to eat?
A: When it's full.

Q: What do you call a tick on the moon?
A: A luna-tick.

Q: What kind of music do planets sing?
A: Neptunes!

Q: What's a light-year?
A: The same as a regular year, but with less calories.

QUIZ ANSWERS
STARS & SPACE

1. True

2. C — Parhelia (sundogs)

3. B — Mesosphere

4. B — Airglow

5. False

6. B — Venus

7. B — Earth passes through comet debris

8. The jet stream

9. B — Atmospheric turbulence

10. False — it contains billions of stars

12

GEAR, GADGETS & TECH

COOL OUTDOOR TECH & GADGETS

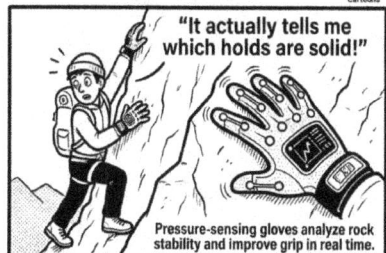

"This thing charges faster than my home outlet!"

Solar smart-packs power phones, radios, and GPS and using ultra-thin photovoltaic fibers.

"It cools itself... and insulates itself?"

Phase-change tent fabrics reflect heat during the day and trap warmth at night.

MIND-BLOWN™ Cartoons

"Trail scouting in ten seconds flat."

Pocket drones map routes and detect hazards long before hikers reach them.

"It actually tells me which holds are solid!"

Pressure-sensing gloves analyze rock stability and improve grip in real time.

MIND-BLOWN™ Cartoons

WEIRD & FUN FACTS GEAR, GADGETS & TECH

MIND-BLOWN MOMENT

🚁 **Solar panels can generate power under a full moon.**
Moonlight is reflected sunlight, and sensitive photovoltaic cells can convert those faint photons into measurable current.

🚁 **High-end compasses can twitch seconds before a distant earthquake.**
Shifting underground stress slightly distorts Earth's magnetic field before the seismic waves arrive.

🚁 **Some climbing ropes momentarily strengthen when friction warms them.**
Heat causes nylon fibers to align tighter, briefly increasing tensile load before returning to normal.

🚁 **Thermal cameras can reveal water flowing inside living trees.**
Sap moving up the trunk creates warmer channels that show up like glowing veins.

🚁 **GPS watches sometimes spike altitude readings during meteor explosions.**
Atmospheric shockwaves disturb pressure sensors long before sound reaches the ground.

🚁 **Titanium cookware can whistle when snow melts inside it.**

Flash-boiling droplets force steam through microscopic metal imperfections at high speed.

🛰 **Carbon trekking poles can detect hollow ground beneath your feet.**
Resonance changes in the carbon shaft vibrate differently over buried voids.

🛰 **Solar lanterns glow brighter in subzero temperatures.**
Cold conditions improve LED efficiency and lower electrical resistance.

🛰 **Some tents bow inward just before a wind gust hits.**
Pressure waves move faster than the wind itself and flex the fabric in advance.

🛰 **High-power headlamps reveal drifting ice crystals in "clear" night air.**
LED beams scatter off microscopic frost nuclei invisible to the naked eye.

🛰 **Ultralight backpack straps can buzz during geomagnetic storms.**
Charged particles induce microcurrents in conductive stitching threads.

🛰 **Certain water filters work faster in icy glacial runoff.**
Fine sediment bonds electrostatically to the membrane surface for cleaner flow.

🛰 **Hiking boots can transmit distant rockfalls through their soles.**
Granite slabs carry low-frequency tremors remarkably well.

🛰 **Metal tent poles can crackle during static-heavy winds.**
Dust-filled gusts electrify the surface and release tiny sparks.

🛰 **Some GPS units lose accuracy near large waterfalls.**
Ionized mist interferes with satellite timing signals.

🐾 **"Dead" lithium batteries often revive when warmed by body heat.**
Temperature increases ion mobility and restores chemical flow.

🐾 **Binoculars can reveal shimmering "heat rivers" at dawn.**
Temperature gradients bend light across valley floors as the sun rises.

🐾 **Compression sacks can inflate by themselves at altitude.**
Lower external pressure draws air through the weave of the fabric.

🐾 **Multitools can form beads of "metal dew" overnight.**
Rapid temperature drops force condensed moisture out of warm steel.

🐾 **Some tents glow faintly when shaken in darkness.**
Static electricity excites fluorescent fibers woven into the fabric.

🐾 **Water bottles can crackle loudly on freezing nights.**
Expanding ice fractures create sharp acoustic bursts inside the plastic.

🐾 **GPS receivers can pick up faint auroral interference.**
Charged particles in polar regions bend and distort satellite signals.

🐾 **Metal mugs can slowly slide across smooth rock in the cold.**
Uneven temperature expansion in the stone creates subtle movement.

🐾 **Camp stoves roar louder at altitude.**
Thin air accelerates fuel flow and changes flame resonance.

🐾 **Certain hiking socks neutralize odor using silver threads.**
Silver ions disrupt bacterial respiration on contact.

🐾 **Climbing cams can ping softly during sudden cold snaps.**
Metal contraction releases tiny amounts of stored spring tension.

Hard-shell coolers can knock from the inside at night.
Warm trapped air contracts rapidly and flexes the insulated walls.

Some lantern mantles glow green in freezing air.
Rare-earth salts ionize differently at low temperatures.

Windproof lighters lean toward cave entrances.
Convection paths pull flame toward available oxygen flow.

GPS trackers drift near iron-rich cliffs.
Mineral-dense rock warps the local magnetic field.

Moisture-wicking shirts can amplify your heartbeat in silence.
Vibrations travel through the fabric and into your ears like a stethoscope.

Certain rope fibers "sing" when weighted on snow bridges.
Cold tension resonates in the sheath with each step.

Camp chairs sink faster into morning soil.
Dew-softened ground loses rigidity until sunlight dries it.

LED lanterns reveal insects invisible in daylight.
Short-wavelength light reflects off ultra-thin wing membranes.

Metal utensils can warm slightly when lightning storms approach.
Electrostatic buildup increases temperature on thin metal surfaces.

Trail radios travel farther during temperature inversions.
Layered air bends signals over mountains and long distances.

Hydration bladders can inflate overnight in humid air.
Moisture diffuses through membranes, equalizing internal pressure.

🐾 **Ice axes can buzz faintly during snow flurries.**
Wind-driven crystals strike the metal shaft rapidly.

🐾 **Dry bags can expand during rapid altitude drops.**
Air pressure outside rises faster than inside, puffing the bag outward.

🐾 **High-lumen flashlights can reveal hidden minerals in canyon walls.**
Iron-rich veins sparkle intensely under specific LED frequencies.

🐾 **Some tents stiffen slightly during solar storms.**
Electrostatic fields cause fibers to repel each other microscopically.

🐾 **Certain boots squeak only at night.**
Cooling tread rubber contracts unevenly in cold air.

🐾 **Knife blades frost first along the edge in subzero weather.**
Thin metal cools quicker and captures airborne ice moisture.

🐾 **Satellite messengers fail more often near volcanic rock.**
Basalt absorbs and weakens high-frequency radio waves.

🐾 **Cooking pots can ring like bells as they cool.**
Metal contraction creates tension that releases in musical pings.

🐾 **Batteries discharge slower in dry snow than in warm rain.**
Moisture-free cold prevents conductive films from forming.

🐾 **High-tech tent fabric can repel dew like tiny ball bearings.**
Hydrophobic coatings increase water's **contact angle** so droplets roll freely.

🐾 **Waterproof jackets glow under UV headlamps.**
Fluorescent dyes illuminate seams and stress points.

🛦 **Gear sheds echo louder in fog.**
Dense air carries sound far more efficiently than dry air.

🛦 **Some compasses tilt unexpectedly in dense forests.**
Iron-rich soil concentrated by roots alters magnetic pathways.

🛦 **Drones rise faster in cold air.**
Dense atmosphere increases rotor lift and efficiency.

🛦 **Synthetic sleeping bags rustle louder at low temperatures.**
Frozen fibers stiffen, amplifying each movement.

🛦 **Trail cameras can catch invisible insect paths.**
Infrared sensors record heat traces too faint for the eye.

🛦 **Grill grates can warp instantly from melted snow.**
Sudden temperature shock twists the metal faster than it can contract.

🛦 **Wrist altimeters jump dramatically when storms approach.**
Barometric pressure plummets before rainfall, simulating altitude gain.

🛦 **Satellite maps misread canyon depth in winter.**
Cold dense air refracts radar beams unpredictably.

🛦 **Certain tents inflate like balloons in strong updrafts.**
Warm canyon winds force pressure buildup beneath the rainfly.

🛦 **GPS signals bounce off cliffs like mirrors.**
Multipath reflections create ghost positions on your display.

🛦 **Premium gloves can feel sticky on dry granite.**
Microporous leather increases friction when humidity is low.

🛦 **Some compasses swing north faster near thunderstorms.**
Electromagnetic pulses temporarily strengthen Earth's field.

🐿 **Ultra-thin ropes glow faintly during friction burns.**
Rapid heating excites nylon molecules into brief luminescence.

🐿 **Rechargeable lanterns flicker in extreme cold.**
Lithium ions slow enough to cause voltage instability.

🐿 **Certain tent fabrics pop sharply during hail.**
Ice impacts flex the membrane faster than it can relax.

🐿 **Hydration tubes freeze from the mouthpiece inward.**
Exhaled moisture condenses first and forms an ice plug.

🐿 **Metal canteens echo differently depending on altitude.**
Air pressure changes the resonance chamber inside.

🐿 **High-grade crampons can spark on quartz-rich rock.**

'Q: What do you call a
bear with no teeth?
A: A gummy bear.'

'Q: How do you tell if a
tree is a dogwood?
A: By its bark.'

MYTHS – BUSTED
GEAR, GADGETS & TECH

MYTHS

Myth #1: "New batteries perform best in the cold."
Fact: Lithium loses ion mobility in freezing temperatures, so a "full" battery can behave dead until warmed by body heat.

Myth #2: "Carbon trekking poles conduct less electricity than metal ones."
Fact: Carbon fiber is a strong electrical conductor — the resin coating only *seems* non-metallic.

Myth #3: "GPS works anywhere outdoors."
Fact: Deep valleys, dense forests, and iron-rich rock can cause "multipath errors," making GPS readings drift unpredictably.

Myth #4: "Expensive tents never collect interior frost."
Fact: Your breath alone contains enough moisture to freeze on *any* fabric when temperatures drop below dew point.

Myth #5: "Water filters remove all harmful particles."
Fact: Most filters can't trap **viruses** or ultra-fine glacial silt unless paired with purification tablets or boiling.

Myth #6: "High-altitude cooking is faster because the flame looks hotter."
Fact: Lower air pressure means water boils at a lower temperature, slowing cooking dramatically despite a strong flame.

Myth #7: "Metal mugs keep drinks hotter near a campfire."
Fact: Thin metal radiates heat quickly — your drink cools faster compared to insulated plastic or double-wall designs.

Myth #8: "Camping lanterns attract insects because of their brightness."
Fact: It's the **wavelength**, not brightness — many LEDs emit at frequencies insects use for navigation.

Myth #9: "A compass always works unless it's broken."
Fact: Nearby electronics, steel tools, stoves, and even a phone battery can subtly pull the needle off true.

Myth #10: "Hiking boots with deep tread prevent slips on wet rock."
Fact: Deep lugs reduce surface contact — slick rock requires softer rubber compounds, not aggressive tread.

Myth #11: "Solar chargers don't work on cloudy days."
Fact: Many panels convert scattered light efficiently — thin-film panels often generate more power in diffuse sunlight.

Myth #12: "Rope is strongest when brand-new."
Fact: Fresh fibers often still contain lubricants from manufacturing; rope reaches peak strength after a brief break-in period.

WEIRD & FUN FACTS

Satellite maps misread canyon depth in winter.
Cold air bends radar beams.
MIND-BLOWN™ Cartoons

Some tents inflate in strong updrafts.
Warm canyon winds build pressure.
MIND-BLOWN™ Cartoons

GPS signals bounce like mirrors.
Reflections create ghost positions.
MIND-BLOWN™ Cartoons

Premium gloves feel sticky on dry granite.
Microporous leather boosts friction.
MIND-BLOWN™ Cartoons

Compasses swing faster near storms.
Electromagnetic pulses strengthen the field.
MIND-BLOWN™ Cartoons

Ultra-thin ropes glow during burns.
Heat excites nylon fibers.
MIND-BLOWN™ Cartoons

LEGENDS
GEAR, GADGETS & TECH

LEGENDS

The Compass That Refused North

Early Arctic explorers told of compasses that would spin endlessly in certain regions, refusing to lock on north. Later research found massive magnetic anomalies under the ice — but the legend insists a few compasses spun even when taken *miles* away from those zones.

The Headlamp That Saw What Eyes Couldn't

A mountaineer in the Italian Alps reported his LED headlamp catching "heat shadows" darting across a glacier — shapes his eyes couldn't see. Scientists suggested optical distortion. Others claim he was the first to witness ultra-rare infrared refraction off moving ice layers.

The Stove That Roared Before the Storm

High-country shepherds in the 1800s spoke of iron cookstoves that would emit loud metal groans hours before mountain storms rolled in. Modern climbers have confirmed the phenomenon: plunging pressure distorts metal sheets, creating eerie metallic warnings.

The Lantern That Wouldn't Go Out

A prospector in the Yukon claimed his kerosene lantern kept burning in winds strong enough to rip tents apart. Locals insisted the flame was protected by a quirk in the lantern's geometry — others believed the prospector stumbled into a perfectly still convection pocket in the storm.

The Rope That Hummed Like a Wire

Early climbers in the Karakoram reported fixed ropes vibrating loudly

211

at night, "singing" across the rock faces with no wind. Later expeditions confirmed it: sudden thermal changes can create tension shifts that make anchor lines hum like guitar strings.

The Knife That Sparked Blue Fire
Shoshone guides spoke of flint knives that gave off blue sparks against certain mountain stones. Geologists eventually traced it to quartzite with a rare crystalline impurity — but the legend insists the sparks appeared even on stones without quartz.

The Watch That Ran Backwards
A 1920s surveyor in Patagonia claimed his pocket chronometer reversed direction for several minutes while he stood atop a windy ridge. Modern theories point to cold-induced gear slip, but mountaineers still call it "the ridge that turns back time."

The Tent That Rose on Its Own
Climbers on Denali told of a tent that lifted from the ground, not from wind, but from a sudden warm updraft so strong it inflated the fabric like a balloon. Later, rangers documented violent convective bursts created by rapid ice-slope heating — a rare but real phenomenon.

The Map That Shifted Overnight
Old boundary survey teams in deep canyon country swore their maps changed subtly at dawn — ridgelines appearing larger, shadows moved, distances altered. It took decades to understand: cold night air refracts light so strongly that canyon shapes look physically distorted at sunrise.

DID YOU KNOW? GEAR, GADGETS & TECH

Did you know high-altitude tents can collect ice *inside* even when temperatures stay above freezing?
Moist breath condenses on cold fabric faster than it melts, creating a thin frost layer that forms long before you notice it.

Did you know a GPS can drift by 50–100 feet when sunlight hits canyon walls?
Heat rising off rock creates refractive "signal mirages" that bend satellite timing just enough to shift your position.

Did you know a metal water bottle can explode its cap off on a sunny snowfield?
Cold water warms rapidly in direct sun, building pressure inside the sealed bottle far faster than the steel expands.

Did you know carbon-fiber trekking poles can hum audibly during certain wind angles?
Crosswinds hit the hollow shaft at its resonant frequency, turning the pole into a low-tuned vibrating chamber.

Did you know ultralight backpacks can inflate slightly during fast elevation changes?
Air pressure outside the pack drops so quickly that trapped interior air swells the fabric like a soft balloon.

Did you know your headlamp can reveal invisible frost floating in "clear" air?
LED wavelengths scatter off micro-ice crystals that don't reflect normal starlight, exposing frozen particles you can't otherwise see.

213

Did you know water filters clog almost instantly in volcanic terrain?
Fine ash particles are so small they seal membrane pores the moment water hits the filter surface.

Did you know metal tent stakes can twist slightly overnight without anyone touching them?
Temperature swings expand and contract the soil unevenly, slowly rotating the stake as the ground shifts.

Did you know power banks can lose over half their output the moment they're set on snow?
Extreme cold slows lithium-ion chemical reactions so dramatically that voltage collapses under load.

Did you know polarized sunglasses can reveal stress cracks in ice that look perfectly solid to the naked eye?
Polarized light filters highlight hidden fracture lines by reflecting differently off stressed ice layers.

Did you know some camping stoves burn *hotter* at high elevation despite thinner air?
Lower pressure makes fuel vaporize faster, enriching the flame even as oxygen decreases.

Did you know climbing ropes can stiffen instantly when exposed to sudden humidity drops?
Moisture evaporates out of the sheath so quickly that the fibers contract like tightening muscle.

STORY MOMENT
GEAR, GADGETS & TECH

STORY
MOMENT

The Ridge That Hummed a Warning

I was halfway up the granite ridge when my GPS suddenly leapt a hundred feet sideways on the screen — a jump so big it made the trail vanish beneath me. At first I thought the satellite connection had dropped, but then my trekking pole started vibrating like a tuning fork, buzzing against my palm with this low, strange pressure-wave hum I'd never felt before. The air went still — no wind, no birds — just that rising hum coming up through the rock.

Seconds later, I heard it: a deep, distant crack echoing through the valley like someone snapping a stone spine in half. My GPS jumped again, and the ridge under my boots shuddered as a massive slab sheared off the cliff across the basin, sending a rockfall cascading out of sight. When the GPS finally re-centered, I realized what had triggered the whole thing: the pressure wave from the collapse had hit the ground beneath me *before* the sound reached my ears.

My pole went silent, settling back into my grip as if nothing had happened at all. I never forgot that moment — not the vibration, not the silence, not the way a simple piece of gear warned me before I even knew what was happening.

Sometimes the mountain tells you something long before the sky does — you just have to be holding the right equipment when it speaks.

NO QUIZ... IT IS BREAK TIME!!

THANK YOU!   HAVE A BLESSED DAY

MYTHS & LEGENDS

"New batteries work better in the cold, right?"

Myth: "New batteries perform best in freezing weather."
Fact: Lithium loses ion mobility in the cold — warming it brings it back to life. Soft morning frost glow.

"Why does my GPS think I'm on on three cliffs at once?"

Myth: "GPS works perfectly anywhere outdoors."
Fact: Cliffs and dense rock create multipath errors that confuse signals. Wide shot with dramatic lighting.

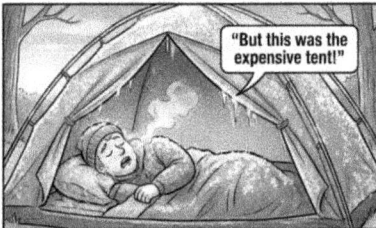

"But this was the expensive tent!"

Myth: "High-end tents never frost inside."
Fact: Your breath alone contains enough moisture to freeze on cold fabric.

"My filter says '99.9%' — that's everything, right?"

Myth: "Water filters remove all harmful particles."
Fact: Most filters can't stop viruses or glacial silt without boiling or purification.

MIND-BLOWN™ Cartoons.